Boosting European Competitiveness

Boosting European Competitiveness

The Role of CESEE Countries

Edited by

Marek Belka

President, Narodowy Bank Polski, Poland

Ewald Nowotny

Governor, Oesterreichische Nationalbank, Austria

Pawel Samecki

Management Board Member, Narodowy Bank Polski, Poland

Doris Ritzberger-Grünwald

Director, Oesterreichische Nationalbank, Austria

PUBLISHED IN ASSOCIATION WITH THE OESTERREICHISCHE NATIONALBANK

Edward Elgar
PUBLISHING

Cheltenham, UK • Northampton, MA, USA

Published by
Edward Elgar Publishing Limited
The Lypiatts
15 Lansdown Road
Cheltenham
Glos GL50 2JA
UK

Edward Elgar Publishing, Inc.
William Pratt House
9 Dewey Court
Northampton
Massachusetts 01060
USA

A catalogue record for this book
is available from the British Library

Library of Congress Control Number: 2016942180

This book is available electronically in the **Elgar**online
Economics subject collection
DOI 10.4337/9781785369322

ISBN   978 1 78536 931 5 (cased)
ISBN   978 1 78536 932 2 (eBook)

Typeset by Servis Filmsetting Ltd, Stockport, Cheshire
Printed and bound by CPI Group (UK) Ltd, Croydon, CR0 4YY

Contents

Contributors

Dan Andrews, Senior Economist, Economics Department, Organisation for Economic Co-operation and Development, France.

Bas B. Bakker, Senior Regional Resident Representative, Regional Office for Central and Eastern Europe, International Monetary Fund, Poland.

Iain Begg, Professorial Research Fellow, European Institute, London School of Economics and Political Science, UK; and Senior Fellow, UK in a Changing Europe Initiative.

Marek Belka, President, Narodowy Bank Polski, Poland.

Konstantīns Beņkovskis, Adviser, Monetary Policy Department, Latviijas Banka and Assistant Professor, Department of Economics, Stockholm School of Economics in Riga, Latvia.

Zsolt Darvas, Senior Fellow, Bruegel, Belgium; Senior Research Fellow, Centre for Economic and Regional Studies of the Hungarian Academy of Sciences, Hungary; Senior Research Fellow, Corvinus University of Budapest, Hungary.

Alain de Serres, Head of Structural Policies Surveillance Division, Economics Department, Organisation for Economic Co-operation and Development, France.

Michał Gradzewicz, Director of the Bureau of Corporates, Households and Markets, Economic Institute, Narodowy Bank Polski, Poland.

Doris Hanzl-Weiss, Research Economist, Vienna Institute for International Economic Studies (wiiw), Austria.

Beata S. Javorcik, Professor of Economics, University of Oxford, UK; Research Fellow, Centre for Economic Policy Research (CEPR), UK.

Anna Kosior, Director, Economic Institute, Bureau for Integration with the Euro Area, Narodowy Bank Polski, Poland.

Krzysztof Krogulski, Economist, Regional Office for Central and Eastern Europe, International Monetary Fund, Poland.

Michael Landesmann, Scientific Director, Vienna Institute for International Economic Studies (wiiw), Austria; Professor of Economics, Johannes Kepler University, Austria.

Ewald Nowotny, Governor, Oesterreichische Nationalbank, Austria.

Brian Pinto, Former Senior Adviser, World Bank; former Chief Economist, Emerging Markets, GLG.

Doris Ritzberger-Grünwald, Director, Oesterreichische Nationalbank, Austria.

Michał Rubaszek, Economic Advisor, Bureau of Applied Research, Economic Institute, Narodowy Bank Polski, Poland.

Pawel Samecki, Member of the Management Board, Narodowy Bank Polski, Poland.

Maria Silgoner, Lead Economist, Oesterreichische Nationalbank, Austria.

Peter Sinclair, Professor of Economics, University of Birmingham, UK.

Klaus Vondra, Economist, Oesterreichische Nationalbank, Austria.

Boris Vujčić, Governor, Hrvatska Narodna Banka, Croatia.

Julia Wörz, Head of Unit, Foreign Research Division, Oesterreichische Nationalbank, Austria.

Linda Yueh, Fellow in Economics, University of Oxford, UK; Adjunct Professor of Economics, London Business School, UK.

PART I

Framing the discussion on the competitiveness challenge

1. Boosting European competitiveness

Marek Belka, Ewald Nowotny, Doris Ritzberger-Grünwald and Pawel Samecki

The topic of competitiveness is more relevant today than ever, for a number of reasons. First, in the years prior to the crisis that emerged in 2008, macroeconomic imbalances built up in several euro area countries. When the crisis erupted, these imbalances aggravated the depth of the recessions and laid bare flaws of the institutional architecture of the monetary union. This raised also the awareness of addressing the underlying competitiveness gaps. Today, competitiveness plays a critical role in returning to a sustainable growth path. In this specific context, 'boosting European competitiveness' refers to the short-term policies necessary to restore a sound mix of strong domestic demand and a high level of external competitiveness.

The second, medium-term challenge is to advance the European integration process so that past experience of diverging economic developments and unbalanced growth models does not repeat itself. 'Boosting European competitiveness' in this context implies the deepening of monetary union, which may involve aspects of economic, fiscal and capital markets union. Given the special role of the banking system in absorbing shocks and in transmitting monetary policy to the economy, the completion of the banking union also plays a crucial role in this respect. While competitiveness is largely a challenge for national policymakers, European policies can and need to deliver their contributions to this overall aim. These policies must also include strong preventive and correcting mechanisms in response to unbalanced growth models. After all, national imbalances threaten the competitive position of the entire region.

Third, at a more global level, we are moving from a bipolar monetary system with two major currency blocs – the US dollar bloc and the euro bloc – to a tripolar world, with China emerging as a new global player. In this context, 'boosting European competitiveness' refers to the challenge of creating a win–win situation in which European producers benefit from integrated production chains that involve Asian economies. This may imply focusing on quality segments in which Europe has a clear competitive advantage.

And finally, in a world of full financial market integration, financial flows move in and out of countries within short periods of time. Countries are potentially confronted with unpredictable exchange rate movements and sudden stops with possibly enormous consequences also for competitiveness. From this perspective, 'boosting European competitiveness' also implies making the export sector of the European Union (EU) more resistant to currency fluctuations. This may call for a high level of diversification of export markets, both in terms of products and geographical regions.

A timely and accurate assessment of the competitive position of regions is a fundamental prerequisite for tackling all these policy challenges. However, traditional, well-established indicators such as macroeconomic price or cost measures alone are unable to provide a comprehensive explanation of recent trade developments. Recent research has led to two quantum leaps in the trade literature, though.

The first finding is that with the increasing technical sophistication of products, quality and customer orientation have become just as important factors of competitiveness as relative costs and prices. In particular, small and open economies in close proximity to their destination markets benefit from their ability to quickly adapt production to changing demands. This allows them to develop quasi-monopoly positions in small niches. Unfortunately, non-price competitiveness is unobservable and hard to express in numbers; often, it is just the residuum, that is, part of export performance that cannot be explained by price factors. Recent research in this area is a welcome step that helps to better understand export patterns.

The second finding is that in an increasingly interconnected world, participation in global production chains is vital. Traditional gross trade data, however, are unable to capture the increasing import content of exports and thus provide a biased picture of trade patterns. Newly developed databases that extract the national value added to exports provide a promising supplement to traditional trade analysis. Again it is especially small and open economies that benefit from division of labour through trade integration, because their size would not allow them to exploit economies of scale. However, the academic dispute on the potential negative side effects and longer-term costs of outsourcing is not yet settled. Many recent examples show that the advantage of close economic ties may quickly turn into risk factors due to contagion effects. Again, recent research has the potential to identify the benefits and risks of global trade integration.

Boosting competitiveness is an issue at the top of the EU's economic policy agenda today. As emphasized above, it is so important because of the challenges facing the EU: both internal ones, linked with the macroeconomic imbalances accumulated in the euro zone and the imperfect institutional construction of the European economic and monetary union (EMU); and external ones, stemming from globalization and financial market integration.

Nevertheless, it is difficult to define and measure competitiveness, in particular when one refers to the competitiveness of the entire economy (not to mention a group of economies, such as the EU). In the online *Concise Encyclopedia of Economics*, Robert Z. Lawrence (1993) compares the notion of competitiveness of the economy to the notion of love or democracy: they all have several meanings and interpretations. When discussing the competiveness of a given country, one may understand it as the economic performance of this country in comparison to others. Alternatively, the notion of competitiveness could be related to its performance in international trade. Another possible interpretation of competitiveness is the efficiency of the use of the available resources.

The lack of a single, common definition makes discussing competitiveness interesting and multilayered. It is also challenging. The chapters in this volume are the finest proof of the complexity of the subject. Their authors presented their different perspectives and points of view on the issue during the conference entitled 'Boosting EU Competitiveness', organised jointly by the Oesterreichische Nationalbank and Narodowy Bank Polski in Warsaw on 15–16 October 2015. The discussions that took place during the conference led to the conclusion that there was no simple answer to the question: 'What can we do to boost EU competitiveness?' In order to provide a comprehensive answer, it is necessary to dig deep and try to distil the factors influencing the competitiveness not only of every EU member state, but also of sectors of their economies and particular enterprises. This is an extremely challenging task, if not impossible. The conclusion is that observations and studies concerning competitiveness are usually not as multidimensional as they should be in order to grasp the whole picture. The chapters reflect this complexity, shedding light on some important factors that should be taken into consideration when analysing competitiveness, not only in the EU.

The first factor is a good understanding of non-price competitiveness. This is an example of a concept that cannot be analysed thoroughly enough on the 'macro level', without going down to the 'micro level'. In particular, it is important to carefully analyse what the attributes of the products are (other than their prices) that make them competitive. It is quality, but also taste and the preferences of the individual customers, that may drive the international success of some products and sectors of the market.

This problem is related to the issue of the difficulties of applying the right data when analysing competitiveness in today's globalized, interconnected world. This refers, for example, to measuring different aspects of the above-mentioned non-price competitiveness, such as finding the best way to quantify innovations and their diffusion. The challenge also concerns the right measurement of the international trade performance, while taking into account the country of origin of value added.

A detailed analysis of the particular countries and industries is therefore a prerequisite for a good understanding of the problems linked with competitiveness and for applying the right policy measures. Consequently, from the point of view of the EU as a whole (which is right to worry about its competitiveness, as the above-mentioned challenges negatively influence its effectiveness and legitimization), it is important to avoid applying the one-size-fits-all approach. In particular, it is clear that a distinction should be made between the challenges regarding competitiveness in the Central and Eastern European (CEE) countries and the competitiveness of the euro zone countries. In fact, in the euro zone, another distinction is needed: between the 'periphery' countries, where the wage increases were higher than productivity growth during recent years, and Germany or the Netherlands, where wages increased less than productivity. The elimination of these misalignments is a priority. In turn, in the CEE countries, the challenge is, in general, the low level of non-price competitiveness that is caused, *inter alia*, by the low level of innovation and weak diffusion of technology and knowledge.

While pondering on possible ways to boost EU competitiveness, we should also bear in mind that the EU as a grouping lacks enough competences in this area to truly influence national economic policies. Another well-known problem concerns the optimal design of the structural reforms that are implemented by the EU member states, as well as difficulties with the proper evaluation of the effects of those reforms.

In conclusion, one needs to be very cautious when analysing EU competitiveness and designing policies aimed at boosting it. The best opportunity to make our own analyses better informed and come up with the best possible conclusions is to get to know the different possible approaches to these issues, such as those presented in this volume.

REFERENCE

Lawrence, R.Z. (1993), 'Competitiveness', in D.R. Henderson (ed.), *The Concise Encyclopedia of Economics*, 1st edition. http://www.econlib.org/library/Enc1/Competitiveness.html (accessed 22 January 2016).

2. Harnessing foreign direct investment to boost economic growth

Beata S. Javorcik

In response to the financial crisis that emerged in 2008, many governments have been looking for ways to restart economic growth. This chapter argues that inflows of foreign direct investment (FDI) may help both advanced and middle-income countries achieve this objective by boosting local research and development activities and by bringing in knowledge and know-how produced elsewhere.

The link between FDI and economic growth was documented a while ago by studies relying on cross-country regressions. In a very widely cited paper, Borensztein et al. (1998) utilize data on FDI flows from industrial countries to 69 developing countries over two decades. They find that FDI contributes to growth to a larger extent than domestic investment. They also show that the contribution of FDI to economic growth is enhanced by its interaction with the level of human capital in the host country. Their results imply that FDI is more productive than domestic investment only when the host country has a minimum threshold stock of human capital. They find no evidence of FDI crowding out domestic investment. Subsequent work in a cross-country setting by Alfaro et al. (2004) has demonstrated that FDI alone plays an ambiguous role in contributing to economic growth, but that countries with well-developed financial markets gain significantly from FDI.

Since cross-country growth regressions are limited in what they can say about the mechanisms behind the link between FDI and economic growth, this chapter will discuss a selection of subsequent studies relying on micro data to elaborate on the channels through which FDI affects growth. The obvious place to start this discussion is to ask which firms undertake FDI. Engaging in FDI is costly because it requires setting up new production facilities, and gaining familiarity with the local laws, regulations and consumers' preferences. Thus, only the best-performing firms – or, to use Dunning's (1988) term, firms that possess 'ownership advantages' – are able to engage in FDI. According to Dunning, these ownership advantages can manifest themselves in the form of new technologies, patents, industry-specific or management know-how, or even well-established brand names. These intangible assets, developed in the firm's headquarters, can easily be transferred to foreign affiliates, and their productivity is independent of the number of facilities in which they are employed. The existence of ownership advantages is reflected in the recent theoretical models of heterogeneous firms, which predict that only the most productive firms can afford the cost of setting up additional production facilities abroad, and hence multinationals come from the upper part of the productivity distribution of firms in their home country (Helpman et al. 2004).

Given these theoretical predictions, it comes as no surprise that multinational corporations are heavily involved in the creation of new knowledge by engaging in research and development (R&D) activities. In 2002, 700 firms, 98 per cent of which were multinational corporations, accounted for 46 per cent of the world's R&D expenditure and 69 per cent of the world's business R&D (UNCTAD 2005). R&D spending of individual firms often exceeds public R&D outlays of individual countries. For instance, in 2003, the gross domestic expenditure on R&D of US$3.84 by the eight Eastern European countries that joined the European Union in 2004[1] was equal to about half of the R&D expenditure of Ford Motor Company (US$6.84 billion), Pfizer (US$6.5 billion), DaimlerChrysler (US$6.4 billion) and Siemens (US$6.3 billion) during the same year, and was comparable to the R&D budget of Intel (US$3.98 billion), Sony (US$3.77 billion), Honda and Ericsson (US$3.72 billion each) (UNCTAD 2005).

While in past decades the R&D activities of multinational corporations used to take place mainly at headquarters, this is no longer the case. A survey of the world's largest R&D investors, conducted in 2004–05 by UNCTAD, revealed that the average respondent spent 28 per cent of its 2003 R&D budget abroad, including in-house expenditure by foreign affiliates and extra-mural spending on R&D contracted to other countries (UNCTAD 2005). In some countries, R&D undertaken by foreign affiliates has accounted for half or more of total business R&D investment. This was true of Ireland where foreign affiliates were responsible for 72 per cent of business R&D spending, Hungary (62 per cent), the Czech Republic (46.6 per cent), the United Kingdom (UK) (45 per cent) and others (see Figure 2.1). The shift of R&D activities abroad has been stimulated by the need to adapt products to the local conditions as well as by cost saving needs.

Similar evidence is available at the micro level. For instance, Guadalupe et al. (2012) show that foreign acquisitions result in more product and process innovation and adoption of foreign technologies in the acquired Spanish firms. The acquired firms also increase their sales and labour productivity faster than the control group. The impact of foreign ownership

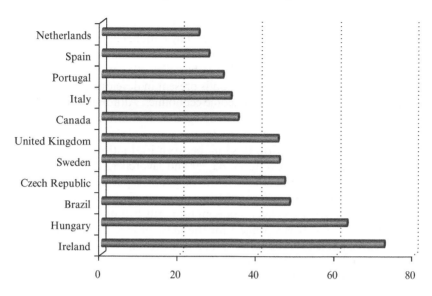

Source: Based on data presented in UNCTAD (2005).

Figure 2.1 Share of foreign affiliates in business R&D, 2003 or latest year available (%)

on plant performance is clearly visible in the Indonesian context where Arnold and Javorcik (2009) find that foreign acquisitions of domestic plants result in a 13.5 per cent productivity boost after three years under foreign ownership. The rise in productivity is a result of restructuring, as acquired plants increase investment outlays, employment and wages. Foreign ownership also enhances the integration of acquired plants into the global economy through increased export and import intensity. As might be expected, divestments by foreign owners partially reverse these gains. Javorcik and Poelhekke (2016) find that a change from majority foreign ownership to domestic ownership is associated with a drop in total factor productivity and is also accompanied by a decline in output, export and import intensity. The latter findings suggest that the benefits of foreign ownership are driven by continuous supply of headquarters services from the foreign parent.

Perhaps the most important aspect from a policy perspective is the evidence suggesting that intangible assets brought to host countries by foreign investors might benefit not just foreign affiliates but also indigenous firms. Such evidence can be found in studies analysing the link between FDI and the quality of exports, product upgrading and total factor productivity. In all cases, the evidence points in the same direction.

A cross-country analysis by Harding and Javorcik (2012) shows a positive association between the sectors treated by national investment promotion agencies as a priority in their efforts to attract FDI, and the quality of exports from those sectors. This analysis, based on 105 countries from 1984 to 2000, indicates that this association is present in developing and emerging markets, though not in high-income economies. Although this analysis cannot distinguish between exports by foreign affiliates and indigenous firms, subsequent studies are able to do so.

Micro-level studies confirm this link between FDI inflows and production upgrading in the host country. Bajgar and Javorcik (2014) find a positive relationship between the unit values of goods exported by Romanian firms and the multinational companies' presence in downstream (input sourcing) industries. This effect is present primarily in industries producing intermediate goods. It is strongest for the most productive and the most sophisticated domestic producers. Similar evidence can be found in Turkey where Javorcik et al. (2015) show that local firms in sectors and regions more likely to supply foreign affiliates are also more likely to introduce more complex products, where complexity is captured using a measure developed by Hausmann and Hidalgo (2009).

There is also a large literature suggesting that domestic firms improve their productivity as a result of interactions with multinationals they supply. The evidence supporting this view comes from a number of countries, including Lithuania (Javorcik 2004), Indonesia (Blalock and Gertler 2008), Romania (Javorcik and Spatareanu 2008) and many others.[2] This improvement may take place because in their quest for higher-quality inputs, multinationals may provide their local suppliers with expertise, training and incentives for quality improvement, and possibly even cooperate on developing new and higher-quality products. Many multinationals subject their potential suppliers to technical audits and expect improvements to performance or product quality as a precondition for receiving a contract. A substantial body of anecdotal evidence suggests that these effects indeed take place. A survey among Czech manufacturing firms discussed by Javorcik (2008) indicates that 40 per cent of Czech suppliers receive some kind of assistance from their multinational customers. This assistance can take the form of employee training (19 per cent), provision of inputs (10 per cent), help with quality assurance (10 per cent) and help with finding export opportunities (7 per cent). Even more remarkably, 50 per cent of domestic firms supplying multinationals report that they had to improve product quality to become suppliers.

These papers documenting the benefits of linkages with multinationals, cited above, are unable to explicitly identify suppliers and instead rely on national input–output matrices to proxy for linkages between industries.

An exception is a study by Javorcik and Spatareanu (2009a), which concludes that while the most productive local firms self-select into becoming suppliers, they also improve their performance as a result of their relationship with a multinational customer. Another study by Javorcik and Spatareanu (2009b), based on the same data, finds that Czech firms supplying multinationals are less credit-constrained than non-suppliers. A closer inspection of the timing of the effect, however, suggests that this result is due to less-constrained firms self-selecting into becoming suppliers, rather than the benefits being derived from the supplying relationship. This echoes the results of the cross-country analysis by Alfaro et al. (2004) that well-developed financial markets may be needed in order to take full advantage of the benefits associated with FDI inflows.

A novel and interesting approach to examining intra-industry spillovers is taken by Kee (2015), who observes business relationships between Malaysian garment producers and their suppliers of intermediate inputs. Her results are consistent with Malaysian firms becoming more productive as a result of sharing suppliers with foreign affiliates.

What does it all mean for policy? Should countries offer preferential treatment to foreign investors? The argument for special treatment of foreign investors is usually based on a market failure. The existence of positive externalities associated with FDI constitutes an example of a market failure and hence could serve as a justification for subsidizing FDI. Nevertheless, given the difficulties associated with assessing the benefits of such spillovers, it might be easy to extend subsidies beyond levels that can be justified based on knowledge spillovers. Haskel et al. (2007) found such evidence for Britain, with foreign investors being offered incentives that exceeded the value of spillovers on a per-job basis. Overpaying is even more likely if similar countries or countries in the same region compete with one another in offering FDI incentives.

Another justification for special treatment of FDI is based on information asymmetries. Indigenous investors, who are better informed about investment opportunities in their country, have no incentive to share this information with potential foreign investors. In such a situation, a capital-importing country would raise welfare by subsidizing foreign capital inflows (Gordon and Bovenberg 1996). However, if the first few FDI projects or entry of a large multinational serves as a signal to other investors that a particular country is an attractive location for FDI, then the justification based on the information asymmetries may apply only to the initial period after opening to FDI, and thus is not relevant for most economies these days.

However, a case may be made for subsidizing information provision to foreign investors, an activity that is rather inexpensive. Recent evidence from 124 countries suggests that investment promotion activities (such as information provision and cutting the costs of complying with administrative requirements) lead to higher FDI flows to countries in which information asymmetries are likely to be severe, and to countries where the administrative burden is high (Harding and Javorcik 2011).

In sum, the findings of the existing literature suggest that FDI inflows can be harnessed to boost economic growth in host countries. Although subsidizing information provision by investment promotion agencies may be warranted, the case for general FDI subsidies is much weaker.

NOTES

1. The group of eight new members included the Czech Republic, Estonia, Hungary, Latvia, Lithuania, Poland, Slovakia and Slovenia. Because the 2003 figures were not available for Lithuania and Slovenia, the 2002 data were used for these countries.
2. For a meta-analysis of studies on productivity spillovers from FDI through backward linkages, see Havranek and Irsova (2011).

REFERENCES

Alfaro, L., A. Chanda, S. Kalemli-Ozcan and S. Sayek (2004), 'FDI and Economic Growth: The Role of Local Financial Markets', *Journal of International Economics* 64(1), 89–112.

Arnold, J. and B.S. Javorcik (2009), 'Gifted Kids or Pushy Parents? Foreign Direct Investment and Firm Productivity in Indonesia', *Journal of International Economics* 79(1), 42–53.

Bajgar, M. and B.S. Javorcik (2014), 'Climbing the Rungs of the Quality Ladder: FDI and Domestic Exporters in Romania', University of Oxford, mimeo.

Blalock, G. and P.J. Gertler (2008), 'Welfare Gains from Foreign Direct Investment through Technology Transfer to Local Suppliers', *Journal of International Economics* 74(2), 402–21.

Borensztein, E., J. De Gregorio and J.-W. Lee (1998), 'How Does Foreign Direct Investment Affect Economic Growth?', *Journal of International Economics* 45(1), 115–35.

Dunning, J. (1988), 'The Eclectic Paradigm of International Production: A Restatement and Some Possible Extensions', *Journal of International Business Studies* 19(1), 1–31.

Gordon, R. and L. Bovenberg (1996), 'Why Is Capital So Mobile Internationally? Possible Explanations and Implications for Capital Income Taxation', *American Economic Review* 86(5), 1057–75.

Guadalupe, M., O. Kuzmina and C. Thomas (2012), 'Innovation and Foreign Ownership', *American Economic Review* 102(7), 3594–627.

Harding, T. and B.S. Javorcik (2011), 'Roll out the Red Carpet and They Will Come: Investment Promotion and FDI Inflows', *Economic Journal* 121(557), 1445–76.

Harding, T. and B.S. Javorcik (2012), 'FDI and Export Upgrading', *Review of Economics and Statistics*, 94(4), 964–80.

Haskel, J.E., S.C. Pereira and M.J. Slaughter (2007), 'Does Inward Foreign Direct Investment Boost the Productivity of Domestic Firms?', *Review of Economics and Statistics* 89(2), 482–96.

Hausmann, R. and C.A. Hidalgo (2009), 'The Building Blocks of Economic Complexity', *Proceedings of the National Academy of Sciences of the United States of America* 106, 10570–75.

Havranek, T. and Z. Irsova (2011), 'Estimating Vertical Spillovers from FDI: Why Results Vary and What the True Effect Is', *Journal of International Economics* 85(2), 234–44.

Helpman, E., M.J. Melitz and S.R. Yeaple (2004), 'Export versus FDI with Heterogeneous Firms', *American Economic Review* 94(1), 300–316.

Javorcik, B.S. (2004), 'Does Foreign Direct Investment Increase the Productivity of Domestic Firms? In Search of Spillovers through Backward Linkages', *American Economic Review* 94(3), 605–27.

Javorcik, B.S. (2008), 'Can Survey Evidence Shed Light on Spillovers from Foreign Direct Investment?', *World Bank Research Observer* 23(2), 139–59.

Javorcik, B.S., A. Lo Turco and D. Maggioni (2015), 'New and Improved: FDI and the Building Blocks of Complexity', University of Oxford, mimeo.

Javorcik, B.S. and S. Poelhekke (2016), 'Former Foreign Affiliates: Cast Out and Outperformed?', *Journal of the European Economic Association*, forthcoming.

Javorcik, B.S. and M. Spatareanu (2008), 'To Share or Not to Share: Does Local Participation Matter for Spillovers from FDI?', *Journal of Development Economics* 85(1–2), 194–217.

Javorcik, B.S. and M. Spatareanu (2009a), 'Tough Love: Do Czech Suppliers Learn from Their Relationships with Multinationals?', *Scandinavian Journal of Economics* 111(4), 811–33.

Javorcik, B.S. and M. Spatareanu (2009b), 'Liquidity Constraints and Linkages with Multinationals', *World Bank Economic Review* 23(2), 323–46.

Kee, H.L. (2015), 'Local Intermediate Inputs and the Shared Supplier Spillovers of Foreign Direct Investment', *Journal of Development Economics* 112, 56–71.

United Nations Conference on Trade and Development (UNCTAD) (2005), *World Investment Report: Transnational Corporations and the Internalization of R&D*, New York, USA and Geneva, Switzerland: United Nations.

3. Correcting external imbalances in the European economy

Michael Landesmann and Doris Hanzl-Weiss

Many of the lower and medium-income European economies (LMIEs)[1] showed rather dramatic deteriorations in their current accounts prior to the outbreak of the financial crisis in 2008–09. Consequently, the question has since been discussed of whether these economies are moving towards a more sustainable path with regard to external balances, and thus competitiveness, in the future. In this chapter we shall examine current account developments in different country groups amongst the LMIEs both prior to the crisis and following it, and analyse structural and real exchange rate developments which might lead to a correction of their longer-term positions with regard to external imbalances.

The main questions of our analysis include:

- What drove the development of current account imbalances before the crisis?
- How has adjustment of current account imbalances occurred after the crisis?
- Can we see signs that external imbalances of Europe's LMIEs are being sustainably corrected?
- What has driven real exchange rate developments since the crisis, and can we rely on these to correct external imbalances in the longer run?

There is a vast amount of literature dealing with the rise of current account deficits before the crisis (e.g., Jaumotte and Sodsriwiboon 2010; Chen et al. 2012; Darvas 2012), the adjustment process thereafter, or both (see, e.g., Gaulier and Vicard 2012; Atoyan et al. 2013; Landesmann and Hanzl-Weiss 2013; Kang and Shambaugh 2015). A number of factors have been explored in great detail.

The main storyline and the most commonly used explanation can be summarized like this (see Atoyan et al. 2013): with the beginning of the euro and thus financial integration, financial flows were facilitated and borrowing costs declined quickly. This resulted in a credit boom leading to sharply increasing imports and widening current accounts deficits. Funds were going to the non-tradables sector in the periphery: into the construction sector in Spain and Ireland; and into excess consumption in Greece and Portugal (Giavazzi and Spaventa 2010; Gaulier and Vicard 2012). Exports were less of a problem in the pre-crisis period (for example, there was rather similar export behaviour in surplus and deficit countries; see European Commission 2012).

The immediate crisis effect comprised a domestic demand compression, and trade collapsed. In the euro area, current account deficits continued to be financed through the TARGET2[2] payment system; thus imports did not have to be reduced radically (Atoyan et al. 2013). In some non-euro countries, the crisis led to problems in refinancing their external liabilities. Hungary, Latvia and Romania had to ask for official international balance-of-payments assistance from the European Union (EU) and the International Monetary Fund (IMF) in late 2008 and early 2009. Poland was admitted to the IMF's Flexible Credit Line in May 2009 to weather the global economic crisis (Forgó and Jevčák 2015). Developments in some of the Central European economies (the Czech Republic, Hungary, Poland, Slovakia, Slovenia) were different from those in most of the other LMIEs in that external imbalances never exploded, trade balances moved prior to the crisis towards zero or became slightly positive, and there was much less need for adjustment in the wake of the crisis.

In this chapter we shall look at these issues more closely. Section 3.1 will examine current account developments over the pre-crisis and crisis periods and Section 3.2 will examine in more detail the different components of the current accounts, with a focus on trade accounts. Section 3.3 will take a closer look at export performance of LMIEs. Section 3.4 will then focus on real effective exchange rates (REERs) and examine by means of a decomposition which factors were responsible for REER developments prior to and after the crisis. We shall also examine to what extent export market share developments are related to REERs. Section 3.5 examines structural developments with a focus on the contributions of tradable and non-tradable sectors to economic growth pre- and post-crisis. Section 3.6 concludes.

3.1 STYLIZED FACTS ON CURRENT ACCOUNT DEVELOPMENTS

In the following we look at the lower and medium-income European economies which encompass the following country groupings: the Southern

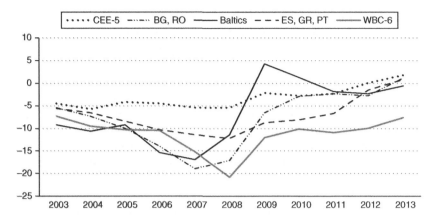

Notes: The Western Balkan countries, WBC-6, comprise Albania, Bosnia and Herzegovina, Macedonia, Montenegro, Serbia and Kosovo. CEE-5 = Czech Republic, Hungary, Poland, Slovakia, Slovenia. BG = Bulgaria. RO = Romania. ES = Spain, GR = Greece. PT = Portugal. wiiw = Vienna Institute for International Economic Studies.

Source: wiiw annual database incorporating national and Eurostat statistics.

Figure 3.1   Current account in % of GDP

EU countries (Greece, Portugal, Spain), the Central and Eastern European new member states (CEE-5: Czech Republic, Hungary, Poland, Slovakia, Slovenia), the Baltic countries ('Baltics': Estonia, Latvia, Lithuania), Bulgaria and Romania, and the Western Balkan countries (WBC-6: Albania, Bosnia and Herzegovina, Macedonia, Montenegro, Serbia, and Kosovo; this group will at times comprise fewer states if there are data problems). As regards time periods, we look at the period before the crisis in 2008 and the period after the crisis.

We start with an overview of current account developments (Figure 3.1): the interesting feature here is the difference between the CEE-5 group and the other LMIE economies. The CEE-5 maintained on average a current account deficit of about 5 per cent of gross domestic product (GDP) continuously during the pre-crisis period. All the other LMIEs experienced sharply deteriorating current accounts reaching levels of between −12 per cent in the Southern EU economies and −20 per cent in the Western Balkan economies.

The crisis led to very sharp corrections in the current accounts in some of the economies (for example, in the Baltics from a position of −17 per cent in 2007 to +4 per cent in 2009; in Bulgaria and Romania from −19 per cent in 2007 to −2.5 per cent in 2010), and in some economies to more gradual but also very substantial adjustments (in the Southern EU economies from −12 per cent in 2008 to +1 per cent in 2014; and in the Western Balkan economies from −20 per cent in 2008 to −8 per cent in 2013).

The literature refers to a 'sudden stop' that initiated these dramatic corrections as foreign net capital inflows slowed dramatically or even reversed as foreign investors were no longer willing to finance such large deficits in the current accounts. The CEE-5 were again an exception as the change in current account positions pre-crisis to post-crisis was relatively mild; however, they also moved from −5 per cent in 2008 into positive territory by 2013. In the next section we examine which components of the current account were responsible for these adjustments during the different phases of the crisis period.

3.2 COMPOSITION OF THE CURRENT ACCOUNTS AND CHANGES DURING THE TWO TIME PERIODS

Figure 3.2 shows the developments in the classical components of the current accounts: the trade balances (exports of goods and services minus imports of goods and services), the primary income accounts (showing the net receipts of factors of production from abroad; in the case of the

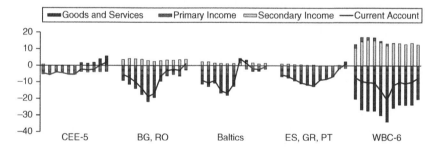

Notes: Components refer to 6th edition of the Balance of Payments (BOP) Manual of the International Monetary Fund as far as available, BOP 5th edition otherwise. Primary income refers to income accounts, secondary income to current transfers. The Western Balkan countries, WBC-6, comprise Albania, Bosnia and Herzegovina, Macedonia, Montenegro, Serbia and Kosovo. CEE-5 = Czech Republic, Hungary, Poland, Slovakia, Slovenia. BG = Bulgaria. RO = Romania. ES = Spain. GR = Greece. PT = Portugal. wiiw = Vienna Institute for International Economic Studies.

Source: wiiw annual database incorporating national and Eurostat statistics.

Figure 3.2   *Composition of the current account of the balance of payments, 2003–13, in % of GDP*

LMIEs this refers mostly to profits made by international companies in these economies which are either repatriated or reinvested) and the secondary income accounts which mostly show the remittance flows from migrants working abroad.

Figure 3.2 reveals important qualitative differences in the developments of these components in the different groups of economies which drive the movements in the current accounts prior to the crisis.

Most importantly, the difference between CEE-5 and all the other LMIE groups of economies: not only did the current account situation not deteriorate in the pre-crisis period in the CEE-5 while it deteriorated very sharply in all the others, but we can see that the striking underlying component is the development of the trade balance, that is, the relative export to import performance. In the CEE-5 the trade balance reached (on average) a zero deficit position even before the crisis, while in all the other economies we see sharply deteriorating trade deficits. In the extreme cases, the trade deficit reached 20 to 30 per cent of GDP.

Another feature which should be pointed out is that the current account deficit, which amounted on average to 5 per cent of GDP in the CEE-5 prior to the crisis, was almost entirely due to a negative primary income balance and reflected the profits earned (and either repatriated or reinvested) by international companies. To some degree this phenomenon is also present in other economies (Bulgaria and Romania; the Baltics; Spain, Greece and Portugal) but not to the same extent.

Finally, we also see the special position of the Western Balkan economies where the extremely large (and persistent, even after the crisis) deficit in trade is partly covered by large surpluses in the secondary income balance which, as mentioned above, is mostly due to remittances from migrants working abroad.

Next we examine the shifts in the different components of the current accounts which took place following the start of the financial crisis, as this should make transparent what accounts for the 'corrections' (from high deficits) in the current accounts which took place following the impact of the crisis. We shall again focus on inter-country differences.

The three panels in Figure 3.3 depict the contributions of the different components to overall changes in the current accounts in three periods: the pre-crisis period (we chose developments over the years 2004–08), the immediate crisis years (2008–09) and the longer period of 'current account adjustment' during the crisis years (2009–13). There is also one additional decomposition in these figures which goes beyond what we had in Figure 3.2, namely that the contribution of the trade balance has been further decomposed into the separate contributions of exports and imports to the changes in the current account positions.

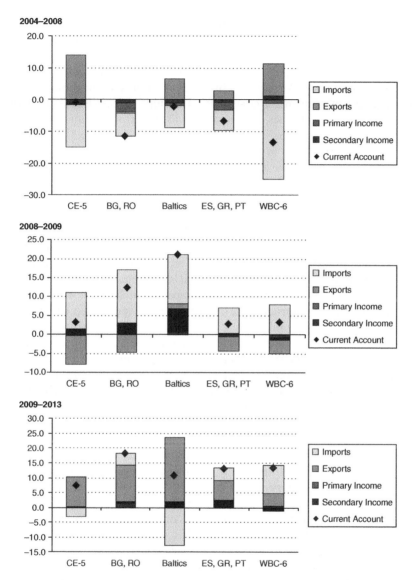

Notes: The Western Balkan countries, WBC-6, comprise Albania, Bosnia and Herzegovina, Macedonia, Montenegro, Serbia and Kosovo. CEE-5 = Czech Republic, Hungary, Poland, Slovakia, Slovenia. BG = Bulgaria. RO = Romania. ES = Spain. GR = Greece. PT = Portugal. wiiw = Vienna Institute for International Economic Studies.

Source: wiiw annual database incorporating national and Eurostat statistics.

Figure 3.3   Changes of current account positions, in % of GDP

The picture which emerges is highly interesting and differentiated across country groups and across the different periods. First of all we see the remarkable shifts in countries which experienced a marked deterioration in the current account positions prior to the crisis (Bulgaria and Romania; Spain, Greece and Portugal; WBC-6) into improved positions in the current accounts during the crisis years. This improvement is also dramatic in the case of the Baltics, which started as well from strongly negative current accounts, but the deterioration (as shown in Figure 3.3) was less dynamic pre-crisis than in the other above-named economies. They then also experienced a move towards a strongly improved current account position in the wake of the crisis.

An interesting point is that the two periods of the crisis years shown in the bottom panels (the immediate crisis impact period, 2008–09, and the period encompassing the entire period following the crisis, 2009–13) differ quite strongly in terms of the nature of current account adjustments. Here the decomposition of the trade balance into contributions from exports and imports is particularly interesting: it shows that the 'improvement' in the current accounts when the crisis impacted in 2008–09 was strongly driven by a sharp contraction of imports, while exports also contracted. Interestingly, in this immediate crisis phase the CEE-5 suffered more strongly from export contraction than the other country groups, presumably because these economies were more strongly linked to cross-border production networks (on this see Francois and Woerz 2009). In the immediate crisis years the primary income balance contributed positively to the recovery of the current accounts in three of the country groups – Bulgaria and Romania, the CEE-5 and the Baltics – presumably because of the dramatic decline of profits made by international firms operating in these countries which most likely lies behind this outcome.

The picture changes dramatically when we compare the immediate crisis impact and the longer period following the crisis: we can see that there is a switch from exports contributing negatively to the current account balance in the immediate crisis years to contributing positively over the entire period of adjustment over the crisis years. This positive contribution of recovering exports is particularly strong in the Baltics, followed by Bulgaria and Romania, and the CEE-5; the contribution of exports was smaller in the Southern EU economies (Spain, Greece, Portugal) and the Western Balkan economies. The strong overall recovery of the economies in the Baltics also meant that imports again started to contribute significantly negatively to current account developments; this feature is shared by the CEE-5 which also had a more stable recovery, but not by the other groups of economies.

To sum up this part of the analysis: we see current account improvements in all LMIE economies following the impact of the crisis, but the degree to which these are the result of improved export performance is quite different in the different country groups. We shall now turn to a more detailed analysis of export performance.

3.3   EXPORT PERFORMANCE

In this section we examine export behaviour before and after the crisis. In the context of our analysis, this variable is important as it indicates whether small- or medium-sized open economies such as the ones in our LMIE sample have the capacity to put their trade balances on a sustainable trajectory. Longer-term trends in the role of exports in domestic production and the development of shares in world markets can serve as important indicators for the trajectory of LMIE economies in terms of competitiveness and sustainability of external accounts. LMIEs are vulnerable in their catching-up phase when import requirements are high to support a technological modernization process, and they face strong competition from both more advanced economies (which sell higher-quality products) and other less advanced economies (which compete on price).

Figure 3.4 shows the share of exports of goods and services in GDP for our country groups. Again, there are significant differences between the country groups, with regard to both pre-crisis and post-crisis developments.

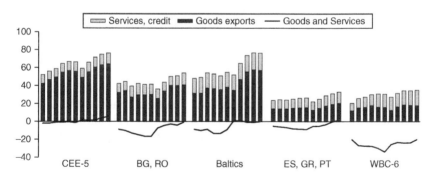

Notes: The Western Balkan countries, WBC-6, comprise Albania, Bosnia and Herzegovina, Macedonia, Montenegro, Serbia and Kosovo. CEE-5 = Czech Republic, Hungary, Poland, Slovakia, Slovenia. BG = Bulgaria. RO = Romania. ES = Spain. GR = Greece. PT = Portugal. wiiw = Vienna Institute for International Economic Studies.

Source: wiiw annual database incorporating national and Eurostat statistics.

Figure 3.4   Export shares (goods and services), 2003–13, in % of GDP

In contrast to all the other groups of LMIE economies, the CEE-5 had a rising share of exports in GDP over the pre-crisis period and this trend continued (after the dip in 2009) over the crisis period. This shows the importance of export activity in these countries, nurtured by a successful integration of these economies in cross-border production networks (see, e.g., Stoellinger and Stehrer 2015). Furthermore the exports-to-GDP ratio has reached a very high level (around 60 per cent prior to the crisis and 65 per cent after that).

The other groups of economies showed a flat development of the exports-to-GDP ratio prior to the crisis and these ratios stayed at relatively low levels: about 40 per cent for Bulgaria and Romania and for the Baltics, and very low ratios of about 20 per cent in the Southern EU group and the Western Baltics; for the latter this is particularly alarming as these are very small economies indeed. Post-crisis there is not much improvement in this ratio in the Southern EU economies and the Western Balkans. An exception amongst the group of economies with formerly very low export ratios, given their size, is the Baltics which substantially increased their export ratios over the crisis period; there was also an improvement in Bulgaria and Romania.

3.4   REAL EFFECTIVE EXCHANGE RATES AND UNIT LABOUR COSTS

Did real effective exchange rates (REER) drive external imbalances (through a loss in cost competitiveness) prior to the crisis? Could cost competitiveness be restored through adjustment of the real exchange rate after the crisis?

Figure 3.5 uses one of the indicators of the 'real exchange rate', namely unit labour costs compared across economies measured in the same currency (that is, euros) and indexed in such a manner that sets the average unit labour costs over the period 1994–2004 to 100. This allows us to see how nominal unit labour costs of different economies (or groups of economies) have moved relative to each other. It is thus an indicator of relative cost competitiveness.

In the top panel of Figure 3.5 a rather familiar picture is shown, that is, the developments of labour unit costs since 2000 of four Southern EU economies relative to those of Germany. This picture has been taken by most commentators as evidence that the Southern EU economies had, over the 2000–08 period, become very uncompetitive, with a relative labour unit cost gap opening up of between 20 per cent and 35 per cent between Germany and individual Southern EU economies. These relative

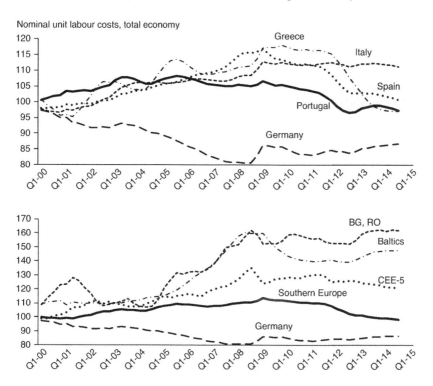

Note: The Western Balkan countries, WBC-6, comprise Albania, Bosnia and Herzegovina, Macedonia, Montenegro, Serbia and Kosovo. CEE-5 = Czech Republic, Hungary, Poland, Slovakia, Slovenia. BG = Bulgaria. RO = Romania.

Source: AMECO (Annual macro-economic) database of the European Commission, authors' calculations.

Figure 3.5   Real effective exchange rates versus (rest of) EU-28 (average 1994–2004 = 100)

unit labour cost developments have been seen as a principal factor behind the very detrimental current account and trade balance developments of the EU's Southern economies over the pre-crisis period. In particular, these have been attributed to very unfavourable relative real exchange rate developments between Germany and this group of Southern EU member countries. It is the purpose of the analysis in this section to be somewhat more differentiated with regard to the role of relative cost (and unadjusted price) measures, as the principal argument behind the critical external imbalances phenomenon in the European economy.

The bottom panel in Figure 3.5 should provide a first signal to be cautious with regard to an unqualified use of such an argument. It shows – in comparison with the bottom panel – that other LMIEs (that is, those of Central and Eastern Europe) experienced much steeper increases in this measure of appreciation of real exchange rates than did the Southern European economies over the pre-crisis period. Both panels also show that all LMIEs did experience – albeit to different degrees – some real exchange rate depreciation over the post-crisis period in relation to Germany. But we shall return to post-crisis REER developments later on.

Given the generally accepted view that REER (as traditionally measured) is considered to be the most relevant variable to judge gains and losses in competitiveness, we want to point the reader to the evidence in Figure 3.6, which shows very little relationship between REER developments and changes in global export market shares. Figure 3.6 shows this relationship for the whole period 2000 to 2014, with respect to the total economy and just the manufacturing sector. For the total economy, Figure 3.7 differentiates further between the two sub-periods, that is, the pre-crisis and post-crisis periods. We can see in these figures that there were groups of Central and Eastern European economies which experienced much stronger REER appreciation over the pre-crisis or the overall period than did the Southern European economies, and nevertheless considerably improved their international market share positions. This should make us cautious with regard to using this measure of competitiveness as a good indicator for changing competitiveness positions, especially in the case of low- and medium-income economies which are – structurally and developmentally – potential catching-up economies.

What is the weakness of the depicted REER indicator? Basically, it is an aggregate indicator of cost competitiveness which explicitly takes account neither of important structural changes (that is, changes in industrial composition and product composition) nor of relative quality improvements of products produced and sold by countries on international markets, both of which are important features of catching-up processes of low- and medium-income economies. We will not dwell on this point any further and refer the reader to the – by now – vast literature on quality assessment and changes in product composition in the international trade literature (see, e.g., Landesmann et al. 2015).

Despite our criticism of the measure of unit labour costs (ULC) as an adequate indicator to assess competitiveness for low- and medium-income economies, we nonetheless move on to a decomposition analysis in order to analyse the roles of the different variables which lie behind ULC developments over the pre-crisis and post-crisis periods. Again, we shall see that interesting inter-country differences emerge from this decomposition analysis.

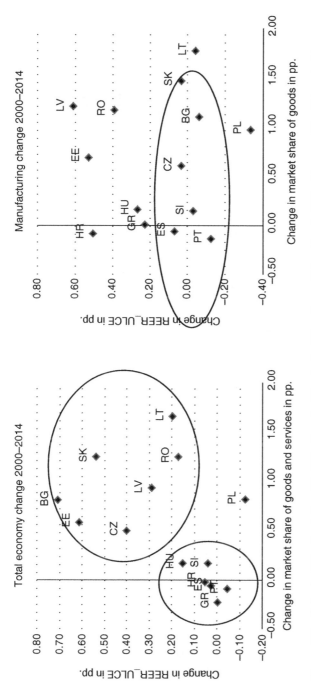

Note: BG = Bulgaria. CZ = Czech Republic. EE = Estonia. ES = Spain. GR = Greece. HR = Croatia. HU = Hungary. LT = Lithuania. LV = Latvia. ME = Montenegro. MK = Macedonia. PL = Poland. PT = Portugal. RO = Romania. SI = Slovenia. SK = Slovakia. REER = real effective exchange rate.

Source: AMECO (Annual macro-economic) database, Eurostat.

Figure 3.6 Change in global export market shares and change in REER

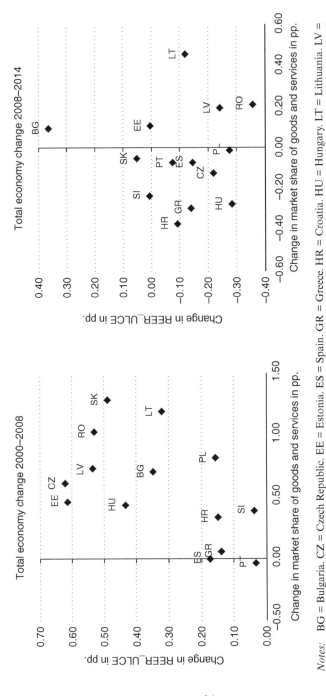

Notes: BG = Bulgaria. CZ = Czech Republic. EE = Estonia. ES = Spain. GR = Greece. HR = Croatia. HU = Hungary. LT = Lithuania. LV = Latvia. ME = Montenegro. MK = Macedonia. PL = Poland. PT = Portugal. RO = Romania. SI = Slovenia. SK = Slovakia. REER = real effective exchange rate. ULCE = unit labour costs in the total economy. ULCM = unit labour costs in the manufacturing sector. pp = percentage points.

Source: AMECO (Annual macro-economic) database, Eurostat.

Figure 3.7 Change in global export market shares and change in REER

The following decomposition formula is applied:

$\Delta\ ULC = -\ \Delta\ Output + \Delta\ Employment + \Delta\ Compensation\ Rate$ (in national currency units, or NCUs) $-\ \Delta\ Exchange\ Rate$

Change in labour productivity | Change in compensation per worker

Exchange rate is defined as *NCU/EUR*. It is clear that for those countries that adopted the euro at a particular juncture or maintained a fixed currency regime in relation to the euro, changes in the exchange rate play no role in driving ULCs.

With regard to Figures 3.8 and 3.9 which depict this decomposition we want to point to the following characteristics of ULC developments in LMIEs over the pre-crisis period (2004–08) and the two periods after that (that is, we again show the immediate impact of the crisis over the period 2008–2010, and then the developments over the longer period 2009–13). First of all, it is important to recognize that nominal exchange rate adjustments played an important role in a number of countries which did not yet belong to the EMU: in Hungary, Poland and Romania there were substantial nominal exchange rate devaluations (relative to the euro) in the immediate crisis phase, and in the pre-crisis period nominal exchange rate appreciations were a significant factor for REER developments in the Czech Republic, Poland and Slovakia.

Secondly, wage developments were important for REER developments, with compensation per employee rising quite strongly in many of the LMIEs prior to the crisis. Notice, however, the difference in the scale of the vertical axis for the Southern European economies from the other economies: while per annum wage growth was high in those economies pre-crisis, wage growth was considerably higher in many of the other economies. Post-crisis, wages fell considerably in Latvia, Lithuania and Greece, and wage growth slowed down or was close to zero in many of the other LMIEs. Interestingly, wages continued to grow quite strongly in Bulgaria.

Thirdly, we come to the third component determining ULC developments, that is, productivity developments, which we want to examine more closely. Here we have the advantage of Figure 3.9 further decomposing labour productivity growth into output growth/decline and employment growth/decline. This decomposition reveals further interesting features that lie behind ULC developments, particularly over the crisis period. Usually, productivity growth should depress ULC growth, hence we would expect the bars in Figure 3.8 to be in negative territory. However, we find that this is not always the case over the crisis period: see the developments in

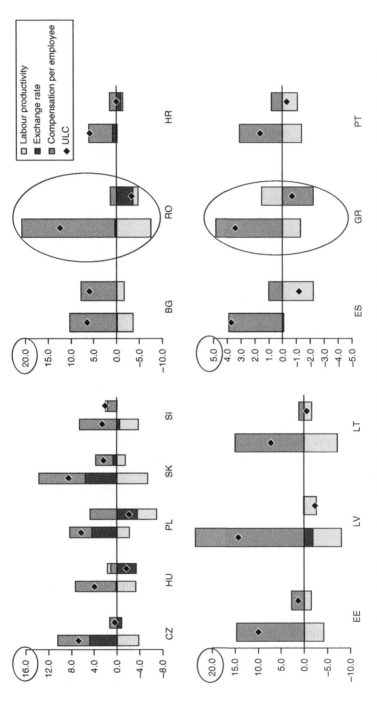

Note: BG = Bulgaria. CZ = Czech Republic. EE = Estonia. ES = Spain. GR = Greece. HR = Croatia. HU = Hungary. LT = Lithuania. LV = Latvia. ME = Montenegro. MK = Macedonia. PL = Poland. PT = Portugal. RO = Romania. SI = Slovenia. SK = Slovakia. REER = real effective exchange rate. ULC = unit labour costs. ULCE = unit labour costs in the total economy.

Source: Ameco (Annual macro-economic) database, Eurostat.

Figure 3.8   Components of ULCs: changes, 2004–08, 2008–10, 2009–13, total economy

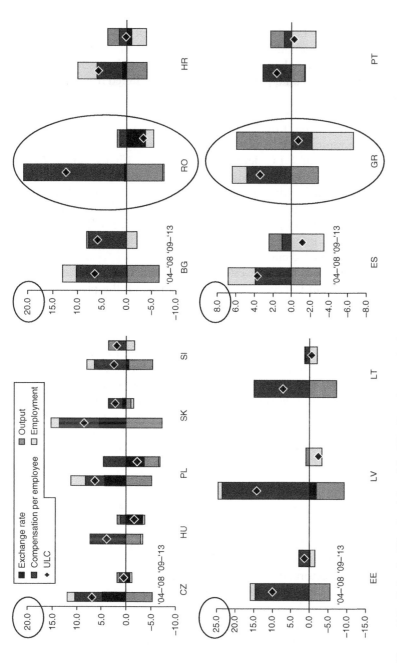

Note: BG = Bulgaria. CZ = Czech Republic. EE = Estonia. ES = Spain. GR = Greece. HR = Croatia. HU = Hungary. LT = Lithuania. LV = Latvia. ME = Montenegro. MK = Macedonia. PL = Poland. PT = Portugal. RO = Romania. SI = Slovenia. SK = Slovakia. ULC = unit labour costs. wiiw = Vienna Institute for International Economic Studies.

Source: wiiw annual database incorporating national and Eurostat statistics.

Figure 3.9   Components of ULCs detailed: changes, 2004–08, 2008–10, 2009–13, total economy

Hungary, Slovenia, Romania, Croatia and Greece in the immediate crisis period (2008–10) and in Hungary, Slovenia and Greece also over the longer post-crisis period (2009–13). Figure 3.9 shows us what lies behind this negative contribution of labour productivity to ULC developments (that is, pushing ULC up rather than down): the three economies mentioned above – Hungary, Slovenia and, particularly, Greece – suffered from severe output contraction which outstripped employment contraction (thus productivity growth was negative) and output contraction was also felt over the longer period in Croatia, Romania, Latvia, Spain and Portugal.

In summary, we want to emphasize two features with regard to what the decomposition analysis of ULC developments showed. Firstly, nominal exchange rate depreciations played a significant role in REER adjustments during the crisis in countries which still had a flexible exchange rate relative to the euro zone. Secondly, the contraction of output induced by the crisis (and accompanying austerity policies) in quite a few of the LMIEs had a significant detrimental impact on ULC developments, basically because output contraction exceeded employment contraction.

For further illustration, let us investigate changes in two countries in particular: Romania and Greece. In the pre-crisis period, the picture of unit labour cost decomposition looks rather similar for the two countries (see Figure 3.9), with strongly growing compensation of employees on the one hand as well as growing labour productivity on the other. However, in the post-crisis period, these two countries differ: in Romania, the exchange rate devalued and productivity improved; in Greece, compensation of employees was cut drastically but productivity did not improve. Investigating productivity trends in more detail, we can see in Figure 3.9 the reasons behind this: in Greece, employment was built up before the crisis; after the crisis, employment fell sharply, but the drop in output was even more dramatic, outpacing employment reductions. Thus, productivity deteriorated and unit labour costs fell only slightly.

3.5   STRUCTURAL STRENGTHS AND WEAKNESSES

The final step in our analysis which we regard as relevant for the topic of correcting for external imbalances refers to structural adjustment patterns with regard to sectoral developments, particularly in relation to the tradable and non-tradable parts of the economies. Instead of analysing the individual sector developments we group them into those which can be classified as tradable – generating exports – and those which are non-tradables and serve only the domestic market. Thus, based on the NACE[3] rev. 2 classification scheme we can differentiate between:

- Those parts in the economy which are tradables: included here is the manufacturing sector (C) as the classic tradable goods sector, and tradable services (TS),[4] including for example financial and insurance activities.
- Those parts of the economy which are non-tradables: these sectors include the construction sector (F), non-tradable services (NTS),[5] with wholesale and retail trade featuring prominently, as well as non-market services.[6]

Figure 3.10 shows the contribution of different sectors to GDP growth over the different sub-periods (pre- and post-crisis). What we can see is that in a number of countries the tradables sector, that is, manufacturing and tradable services, contributed strongly to growth, while in others the contributions of non-tradables, that is, construction as well as non-tradable services, were much more pronounced.

Prior to the crisis (that is, looking at the 2004–08 period), we can see that tradables played a major role in economic growth in the CEE-5, whereby manufacturing provided the strongest impetus, followed by the non-tradable services (NTS) sector and the tradable services (TS) sector. Also in Bulgaria and Romania as well as in the Baltics the contributions of manufacturing and tradable services were quite pronounced, but in these countries non-tradable services played the major role in overall growth. We can also see a major contribution of the construction sector to growth. In the Southern EU countries non-tradable services contributed most to growth, followed by tradable services and non-market services. Manufacturing, on the other hand, played a minor role. We can thus speak of a pattern of sectoral development biased towards non-tradables in these countries. What has happened after the crisis? Have these structural developments, which in some countries had disfavoured the tradables sector prior to the crisis, been reversing?

In the post-crisis period (2008–13), taking the CEE-5 first, growth returned to all sectors of the economy, but again manufacturing became the principal growth driver. Thus the CEE-5 continued their pre-crisis development path with the principal tradable sector playing the most important role for economic growth. In the other countries, construction took a heavy blow of adjustment and saw a prolonged period of negative performance. In the Baltics the manufacturing sector started to play a more important role in economic growth compared to the pre-crisis period. On the other hand, in Bulgaria and Romania growth was on average low across sectors and did not include manufacturing. The Southern countries show an even less promising picture. In these countries, manufacturing suffered (apart from construction) most from the crisis, and could not

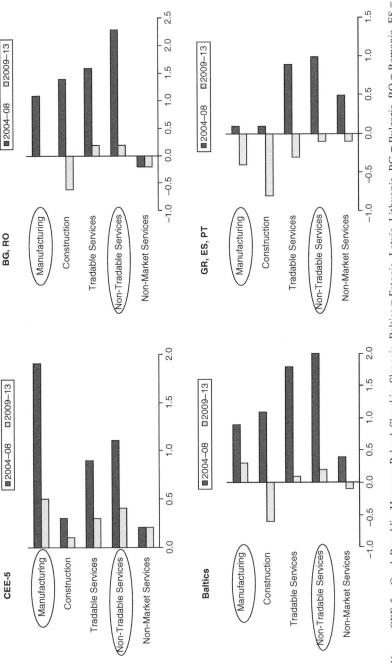

Note: CEE-5 = Czech Republic, Hungary, Poland, Slovakia, Slovenia. Baltics = Estonia, Latvia, Lithuania. BG = Bulgaria. RO = Romania. ES = Spain. GR = Greece. PT = Portugal.

Source: wiiw Annual Database incorporating national and Eurostat statistics, authors' calculations.

Figure 3.10 Contributions to GDP growth by sectors, percentage points 2004–08 and 2009–13 (from constant prices)

recover. There is thus no evidence that the structural bias in favour of non-tradable services and non-market services was being corrected. However, these aggregated data do mask certain adjustment processes that have taken place at the country level. In Greece, despite showing a sad overall picture, as shown by negative contributions to growth of all sectors of the economy, non-tradable services did make the largest contribution to GDP contraction. In Spain and Portugal, on the other hand, construction did adjust most, while non-tradable services (and in Spain non-market services) started to grow again.

3.6   CONCLUSIONS AND POLICY IMPLICATIONS

In this chapter we have emphasized two issues in particular:

- The problem of 'structural' external imbalances in the European economy is not resolved, despite the evidence of a closure of current account gaps in LMIEs during the crisis.
- There is very considerable heterogeneity across groups of LMIEs with regard to various developments which determine whether the external imbalances problem will be resolved in the longer run.

Let us review the evidence presented in this chapter in more detail. First, what we called the 'structural current accounts problem' has relevance in the European economy for countries both inside and outside the economic and monetary union. 'Structural' refers here in particular to persistent weakness of the tradable sector, and it is this weakness which has led to the build-up of considerable external debt in quite a few country groups of Europe's periphery. Reasons for this weakness are manifold: in some country groups it can be traced back to phases of considerable de-industrialization from which these economies did not recover. In some of these and in other economies, this weakness became entrenched by a strong inflow of capital invested predominantly in non-tradable sectors, leading to a spiralling negative impact on the competitiveness of the tradable sector via real exchange rate revaluations. While these developments have taken place, we have also witnessed that there were strong processes of agglomeration of manufacturing activity at work in the European economy (the development of what has been termed the 'Central European manufacturing core', encompassing Germany, Austria, the Czech Republic, Slovakia, Hungary and Poland; see Stoellinger and Stehrer 2015; Landesmann et al. 2015), and these tendencies have made it significantly more difficult for peripheral countries to redevelop sufficient competitive export capacity in the manufacturing sector.

The evidence presented in this chapter has shown that these tendencies in the most vulnerable countries of Europe's periphery (the South and Southeast) have not been significantly reversed in the course of the crisis. In fact, in quite a few of these the tradable sector (manufacturing in particular) has suffered more than the average economy from contraction. This, in turn, is likely to have hysteretic (that is, long-term capacity) effects on the ability of these economies to close current account gaps in the future.

Second, in a detailed analysis of real exchange rate developments, both over the longer term and in the course of the crisis, we have shown that the interpretation of real exchange rate developments with regard to competitiveness requires great caution. There is the question of causality: there is evidence that some economies experienced phases of rapid real exchange rate appreciations without losing competitiveness, and in fact gained considerably in global market shares. This is due to these economies benefiting from considerable structural upgrading of their export sectors, and real exchange rate appreciations were the consequence of such (structural and quality) improvements. Longer-term real exchange rate developments, as traditionally measured, are hence poor predictors of whether a country will improve or lose its market share position in international markets if one ignores the underlying potential of structural improvements. In addition, in a detailed decomposition of real exchange rate developments we have pointed to the potential negative impact which output and employment contraction (which are also important drivers of real exchange rates in the post-crisis period) could have on the longer-term competitiveness of tradable sectors in these economies.

The policy implications of the analysis conducted in this chapter are the following. Countries which suffer from longer-term 'structural' external imbalances have to strongly focus their policy attention on a recovery of the tradable sector. This is not simply a function of real exchange rate adjustments, as the upgrading and expansion of export capacities requires strong investment activities in the tradable sector. This can be assisted by foreign direct investment, but since these flows have become thinner in the post-crisis period (see Hunya 2015), other domestic and EU policy instruments have to be used. We emphasize in other contributions (see, e.g., Landesmann 2015a, 2015b) the use of industrial policy instruments which have to be tailored to the specific requirements of Europe's peripheral economies. While there is a renewed emphasis in the European policy debate on industrial policy which has drawn lessons from negative aspects of 'old industrial policy' (see European Commission 2005), most current proposals at the EU level on industrial policy are aimed at improving the performance of Europe's advanced economies in higher-tech sectors and insufficient attention has been given to the specific requirements of LMIEs in this respect. Combined with the use of innovative industrial policy instruments there has to be an emphasis on institutional upgrading so that industrial policy intervention might show positive rather than negative results (on this, see Stoellinger and Holzner 2016). Furthermore, we would argue that concern about real exchange rate developments is still valid, but this has to be directed towards a joint sustained move towards supply-side improvements (that is, targeting structural change and productivity improvements) as well as a consideration of balanced wage–productivity and human capital developments. Income policies together with education, training and labour market policies should be part of a targeted policy which aims at competitive real exchange rate developments and not simply wage setting. Finally, any reforms of capital markets or policies oriented towards attracting foreign direct investment should carefully consider that a focus has to be the allocation of capital towards (and access to finance of) the tradable sector, and avoid repetition of distorting capital allocations towards non-tradable activities.

NOTES

1. We refer here to member countries within the European Union in Southern and Central and Eastern Europe as well as candidate and prospective candidate countries in Southeast Europe.
2. TARGET = Trans-European Automated Real-Time Gross Settlement Express Transfer system.
3. NACE = Nomenclature statistique des Activités économiques dans la Communauté Européenne; statistical classification of economic activities in the European Community.
4. Tradable services (TS) include: Transportation and storage (H), Information and communication (J), Financial and insurance activities (K) and Professional, scientific and technical activities (M).
5. Non-tradable services (NTS) include: Wholesale, retail trade, repair of motor vehicles (G), Accommodation and food service activities (I), Real estate activities (L), Administrative and support service activities (N), Arts, entertainment and recreation (R), Other service activities (S), as well as Activities of households as employers and for own use (T).
6. Non-market services include: Public administration and defence, compulsory social security (O), Education (P), Human health and social work activities (Q).

REFERENCES

Atoyan, R., J. Manning and J. Rahman (2013), 'Rebalancing: Evidence from Current Account Adjustment in Europe', IMF Working Paper WP/13/73.
Chen, R., G.M. Milesi-Ferretti and T. Tressel (2012), 'External Imbalances in the Euro Area', IMF Working Paper WP/12/236.

Darvas, Z. (2012), 'Intra-Euro Rebalancing is Inevitable, but Insufficient', Bruegel Policy Contribution, Issue 2012/15.

European Commission (2005), 'Implementing the Community Lisbon Programme: A Policy Framework to Strengthen EU Manufacturing – Towards a more Integrated Approach for Industrial Policy', COM(2005) 474 final.

European Commission (2012), 'Current Account Surpluses in the EU', European Commission DG ECFIN, European Economy, 9/2012.

Forgó, B. and A. Jevčák (2015), 'Economic Convergence of Central and Eastern European EU Member States over the Last Decade (2004–2014)', European Commission DG ECFIN, Discussion Paper, 001/July 2015.

Francois, J. and J. Woerz (2009), 'The Big Drop: Trade and the Great Recession', VoxEU, Centre for Economic Policy Research (CEPR), London. http://www.voxeu.org/article/big-drop-trade-and-great-recession.

Gaulier, G. and V. Vicard (2012), 'Current Account Imbalances in the Euro Area: Competitiveness or Demand Shock', Banque de France, Quarterly Selection of Articles, No. 27. https://www.banque-france.fr/fileadmin/user_upload/banque_de_france/publications/1-Current_account_imbalances_QSA27_Autumn2012_internet.pdf.

Giavazzi, F. and L. Spaventa (2010), 'Why the Current Account may Matter in a Monetary Union: Lessons from the Financial Crisis in the Euro Area', CEPR Discussion Papers, No. 8008.

Hunya, G. (2015), 'Recovery in the NMS, Decline in the CIS', wiiw FDI-Report, No. 2015-06.

Jaumotte, F. and P. Sodsriwiboon (2010), 'Current Account Imbalances in the Southern Euro Area', IMF Working Paper, WP/10/139.

Kang, J.S. and J.C. Shambaugh (2015), 'The Rise and Fall of European Current Account Deficits', European Policy, Sixty-First Panel Meeting, Latvijas Banka.

Landesmann, M. (2015a), 'Structural Dynamics of Europe's Periphery – Which are the Main Issues?', *Journal of Economic Policy Reform*, Special Issue, 2015, 202–8.

Landesmann, M. (2015b), 'Industrial Policy: Its Role in the European Economy', in M. Mazzucato, M. Cimoli, G. Dosi, J.E. Stiglitz, M.A. Landesmann, M. Pianta, R. Walz and T. Page, 'Which Industrial Policy Does Europe Need', *Intereconomics* 50(3), 133–8.

Landesmann, M. and D. Hanzl-Weiss (2013), 'Structural Adjustment and Unit Labour Cost Developments in Europe's Periphery: Patterns Before and During the Crisis', wiiw Research Reports, No. 390.

Landesmann, M., S.M. Leitner and R. Stehrer (2015), 'Competitiveness of the European Economy', wiiw Research Reports, No. 401.

Stoellinger, R. and M. Holzner (2016), 'State Aid and Export Competitiveness in the EU', *Journal of Industry, Competition and Trade* (first online: 14 March 2016), 1–34. DOI 10.1007/s10842-016-0222-3.

Stoellinger, R. and R. Stehrer (2015), 'The Central European Manufacturing Core: What is Driving Regional Production Sharing?', FIW Research Report 2014/15 No. 02.

PART II

The various dimensions of competitiveness

4. New indicators of competitiveness: the Austrian perspective

Doris Ritzberger-Grünwald, Maria Silgoner and Klaus Vondra

Numerous traditional data sources are available to investigate the competitiveness position of countries, covering price and cost factors, customs tariffs, infrastructure, the ease of doing business or international trade balances. Several synthetic indicators aim at summarizing this vast amount of information to produce country rankings. Very often, however, these traditional indicators or rankings deliver only an incomplete and partial explanation for patterns of market shares or export growth and, more generally, the export success of countries.

Recent research on competitiveness has generated several new indicators with the explicit goal to simplify, harmonize and condense the large variety of available indictors. One strand of research has the central objective to improve the comparability of indicators across goods and services, across different sectors or across firms and countries. For example the adjustment for non-price factors such as quality or taste is essential in order to be able to assess the competitiveness of goods of different quality and sophistication (see, e.g., Benkovskis and Wörz 2015).

A second strand of research reflects the fact that the production of many common products is scattered all over the world today. In fact, globalization has reached unprecedented levels: about 60 per cent of world merchandise trade is trade in components. The international fragmentation of production has reshaped the implications of world trade for individual countries. Today the competitive strength of a country is crucially determined by its role within global value chains (GVCs).

While GVCs are not new, it took more than a decade to develop a deeper understanding of this phenomenon, so that the awareness of GVCs is rather new in economic analysis and the political debate.[1] This awareness also requires new indicators that reflect changes in the global production processes (see, e.g., Timmer 2012). Actually the term 'global value chain' is somewhat misleading, as a chain reflects a linear concept, while trade links today look more like a web. Yet it is not only a country's level of integration into GVCs that matters, but also its position within a GVC. We know from the literature (e.g., De Backer and Miroudot 2014) that economic activity in most EU (European Union) countries is moving upstream, that is, away from the final consumer towards stages such as product innovation or initial concepts and designs. By contrast, several Southern and Eastern European countries show a development toward more downstream activities, such as final assembly.

For small, open economies, factors such as non-price competitiveness and the cross-border integration of production chains are especially important. We will thus illustrate, through the example of Austria, the multiple dimensions of competitiveness and the value added of novel competitiveness indicators.

4.1 SOME STYLIZED FACTS ABOUT AUSTRIA

Austria is a high-income country with 8.5 million inhabitants. At €34 900, Austria recorded the fourth-highest level of gross domestic product (GDP) in purchasing power parity (PPP) per head in the EU in 2014, but in absolute terms, GDP in Austria accounts only for 0.6 per cent of world GDP. Thus, from a global perspective, Austria is a very small country. As such, Austria has a comparatively limited domestic market. But Austria has the big advantage of being located in the heart of Europe. To exploit this geographical advantage, firms have entered new markets and developed new, innovative products. At the same time, economic policy has provided adequate overall business conditions for both domestic and foreign capital.

As a result, international markets have been open to Austrian products, offering new and huge sales markets. Today more than half of the goods and services produced in Austria are sold abroad, branded with the label 'Made in Austria'. Although Austria is a well-known tourist destination – almost 15 per cent of GDP can be allocated to tourism and leisure services – goods exports clearly exceed services exports, accounting for a share of more than 70 per cent of total exports.

There is no doubt that Austria is one of the major beneficiaries of the European integration process, and this is largely related to its increasing trade integration: in 2014, about half of Austria's goods exports went to euro area countries,[2] thus remaining unaffected by changes in the euro's exchange rate. Almost 70 per cent of all Austrian goods exports go to the EU, thus benefiting from the removal of trade barriers.

With the fall of the Iron Curtain and the subsequent enlargement of

% of total nominal exports of goods

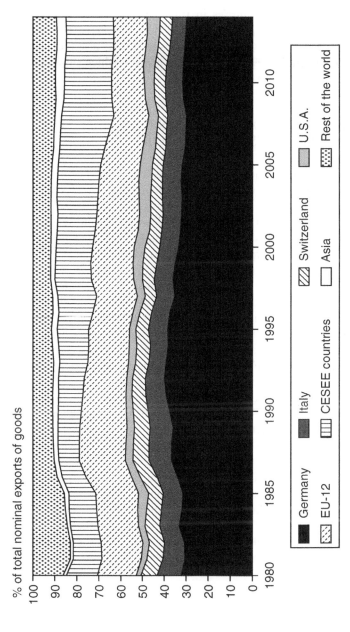

Note: Asia = China, Japan, Korea. EU-12 = Belgium, Denmark, Greece, Finland, France, Ireland, Luxembourg, Netherlands, Portugal, Spain, Sweden, United Kingdom. CESEE = Albania, Belarus, Bosnia and Herzegovina, Bulgaria, Croatia, Czech Republic, Estonia, Hungary, Moldova, Lithuania, Latvia, Montenegro, Poland, Romania, Republic of Serbia, Russia, Slovakia, Slovenia, Ukraine.

Source: Statistics Austria.

Figure 4.1 Regional pattern of Austrian goods exports 1980–2014: exports as a percentage of total nominal exports of goods

the EU and the euro area, Austria moved from the edge of Europe back to the centre. The share of goods exports to Central, Eastern and South-Eastern European (CESEE) countries in total goods exports increased from 14 per cent in 1995 to 22 per cent in 2014 (Figure 4.1). At the same time the share of imports from CESEE countries to Austria also increased markedly, from 9 per cent in 1995 to 19 per cent in 2014, which shows that trade integration works in both directions.

4.2   A CHANGING WORLD NEEDS NEW COMPETITIVENESS INDICATORS

As production processes are increasingly fragmented across borders, the nature of international trade is changing fundamentally. Newly developed databases on value added trade allow us to investigate these issues for the first time. For Austria, the data suggest the following: despite relatively high labour costs, Austria has become increasingly integrated into the value chains that connect Central European countries.

This is illustrated for example by an indicator recently developed within the framework of the Competitiveness Network (CompNet) of the Eurosystem: the index on participation in GVCs (Karadeloglou et al. 2015) complements traditional openness indicators by measuring the importance of global supply chains for a country. This index is very high for several CESEE countries, such as the Czech Republic, Hungary, Slovakia, Slovenia and Poland. But, as Figure 4.2 shows, Austria ranks right after these countries.

While Austria currently benefits from this high level of trade integration, the academic dispute on the potential longer-term costs (catchphrase: 'bazaar economy') is not yet settled. As countries in the CESEE region are catching up, products from CESEE are increasingly competing also with Austrian products.

Take for example the European automobile cluster, spreading from Germany and Austria to the Czech Republic, Hungary, Poland and Slovakia. Within this cluster, Austrian companies deliver highly specialized vehicle parts that require a high level of expertise and innovation. However, the Austrian producers are losing ground in terms of market share in the main assembling market, namely Germany (Figure 4.3).

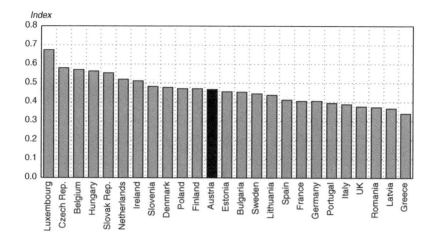

Source: CompNet (European Central Bank).

Figure 4.2 Participation in global value chains, 2011 (index)

4.3 TRADITIONAL COMPETITIVENESS INDICATORS MISS IMPORTANT INFORMATION

Economists have substantial information regarding cost and price developments. However, research has shown that these indicators can only partly explain export and market share developments. Rather it is the unobserved part – namely, non-price competitiveness – that increasingly explains the export performance of countries. Non-price competitiveness comprises factors such as market power, quality, marketing or networking success, and these are clearly key strengths of the Austrian export industry. As a small economy, Austria will never be able to exploit economies of scale to a large extent by entering mass production. Instead, Austrian companies have chosen a different route: they have specialized in high-quality niches and deliver highly sophisticated and costumer-tailored products. In these market segments, quality competitiveness is more important than price competitiveness.

Defending one's position requires steady investment in technological development and a high level of flexibility to adapt to changing demand. Austrian firms are world market leaders in the production of machines and machine parts, cars and equipment, and green technologies. At the

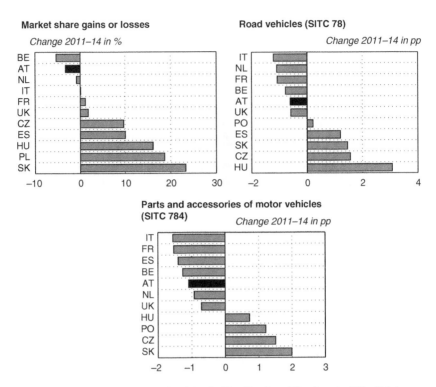

Note: SITC = Standard International Trade Classification. AT = Austria. BE = Belgium. CZ = Czech Republic. ES = Spain. FR = France. HU = Hungary. IT = Italy. NL = Netherlands. PL = Poland. SK = Slovakia. UK = United Kingdom.

Source: Oesterreichische Nationalbank, Eurostat.

Figure 4.3   *Market share development in Germany*

same time, Austrian companies are known for developing innovative production processes, for example in tunnel construction, track laying or in framework technologies.

To be successful in exports, offering good quality is at least as important as being price competitive. Unfortunately, non-price competitiveness is hard to express in numbers; often, it is just the residuum, i.e. that part of export performance that cannot be explained by price factors. Research in this area can help to better understand export patterns.

Again, newly developed data help in illustrating this aspect of competitiveness. The 'goods export sophistication index' (see Figure 4.4 and Karadeloglou et al. 2015) is high for a given country when it exports primarily goods that are also exported by rich countries. In a ranking

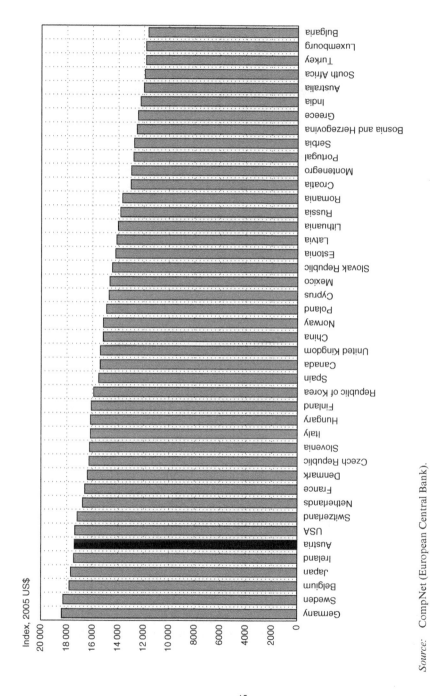

Source: CompNet (European Central Bank).

Figure 4.4 Goods export sophistication index (in 2005 US$)

45

of more than 50 OECD (Organisation for Economic Co-operation and Development) countries, Austria ranks in sixth-highest position, indicating its focus on rather sophisticated goods.

A broader definition of competitiveness goes beyond product quality and – referring to Aiginger (2016) – covers five more general factors: innovation, education, the social system, institutions and environmental ambition. Partly, these capabilities are difficult to trace; however, there are attempts, like the World Bank's *Doing Business Report*, which collects dozens of soft indicators to produce country rankings. Its 2015 edition ranks Austria 21st among 189 participating countries; Austria is thus among the top five euro area countries in this ranking (World Bank 2015). An alternative Eurostat ranking of various factors of life satisfaction puts Austria in the second-best position within the euro area (Eurostat 2015). We acknowledge, however, that these kind of summary indicators share a lack of scientific foundation. While several of the covered sub-indices matter individually for a country's competitiveness, there is usually no empirical proof of the predictive power for exports or market shares.

4.4 CONCLUSION

It is non-price competitiveness and locational advantages that, especially, help to explain the overall strong performance of Austrian exports in the last two decades. Its geographical position and its close economic and historical ties to the CESEE countries offered Austria great opportunities within Europe. New trade indicators in the context of GVCs show the strong integration of Austria with the former Central and Eastern European countries; together with Germany, they form a central trade cluster.

However, venturing into new markets and regions also requires ample financing from banks that are experienced enough to properly assess and price the associated risks. The expansion of Austrian companies into CESEE was preceded by an expansion of Austrian banks into the region, supporting the integration process of the manufacturing industries.

Looking ahead, the challenge for this region, and hence also for Austria, lies in maintaining or even strengthening its acquired position in terms of the worldwide competition. A promising strategy may be to venture into new markets such as those in Asia, which so far play only a minor role for Austria. However, such a strategy also requires a high level of flexibility to adapt to the rapidly changing global trends, as the recent slowdown of activity in Asia illustrates.

NOTES

1. As an anecdotal remark, the VoxEU eBook on the major trade collapse by Baldwin and Evenett in March 2009 (Baldwin and Evenett 2009) makes only two references to global value chains, whereas another VoxEU eReport published by Baldwin on almost the same topic a mere eight months later, in November 2009 (Baldwin 2009), features this factor prominently.
2. Austria's most important trading partner by far is Germany, accounting for a share of close to 30 per cent of Austria's total goods exports. Next in the ranking are Italy, the United States, Switzerland and France.

REFERENCES

Aiginger, K. (2016), 'Deficits and Strengths in Austrian Competitiveness', FIW Policy Brief No 29.

Baldwin, R. (ed.) (2009), 'The Great Trade Collapse: Causes, Consequences and Prospects', VoxEU.org Report. http://www.voxeu.org/sites/default/files/great_trade_collapse.pdf.

Baldwin, R. and S.J. Evenett (eds) (2009), *The Collapse of Global Trade, Murky Protectionism, and the Crisis: Recommendations for the G20*, VoxEU.org Book. http://www.voxeu.org/epubs/cepr-reports/collapse-global-trade-murky-protectionism-and-crisis-recommendations-g20.

Benkovskis, K. and J. Wörz (2015), 'Made in China – How Does it Affect Measures of Competitiveness?', European Central Bank Working Paper 1787.

De Backer, K. and S. Miroudot (2014), 'Global Value Chains Reshape our Policy Thinking', CompNet Policy Brief 6, Frankfurt: European Central Bank.

Eurostat (2015), 'Facts and Views about Quality of Life in the EU', Eurostat News Release 94/2015.

Karadeloglou, P., K. Benkovskis (eds) and the CompNet Task Force (2015), 'Compendium on the Diagnostic Toolkit for Competitiveness', European Central Bank Occasional Paper 163.

Timmer, M. (ed.) (2012), 'The World Input–Output Database (WIOD): Contents, Sources and Methods'. http://www.wiod.org/publications/source_docs/WIOD_sources.pdf.

World Bank (2015), *Doing Business 2015. Going Beyond Efficiency*, Washington, DC: World Bank Group.

5. Globalization and growth: the case of China

Linda Yueh

The Chinese economy has performed remarkably well since the adoption of market-oriented reforms in 1978. The popular perception is that China is a phenomenally successful economy. China's record, however, may mask structural economic problems. Moreover, entry into the World Trade Organization (WTO) has brought new opportunities, but has also introduced risks as China increases its integration into the global economy. The progress and nature of market-oriented reforms of the economy will also play an important role in its growth prospects; that is, China must now address large portfolios of non-performing loans (NPLs) held by state-owned commercial banks (SCBs), rising unemployment in various forms, and the restructuring of inefficient state-owned enterprises (SOEs), to name a few. All this casts doubts on the sustainability of China's growth strategy.

This chapter starts with a review of China's economic reform strategy, tracing today's challenges to the sequencing of reform by going from 'easy to hard' measures. This is followed by an evaluation of the determinants of growth in the context of WTO accession. Based on the identification of the benefits and costs of globalization, the chapter posits that global integration may be the best remedy for resolving the structural problems in the Chinese economy, and concludes with some summary assessments.

5.1 CHINA'S PATH TO ECONOMIC REFORM

The end of the Cultural Revolution in 1976 revived two competing forces: institutional centralization, and accelerated growth, which requires decentralization (Riskin 1987). The reform plan adopted in 1978 to deal with the imbalances inherent in the economy was implemented in the urban areas from the mid-1980s, eventually leading to WTO accession (Yueh 2012).

China opted for a 'dual-track' reform path to address both the planned and the market part of the economy. As we will see, this incrementalist or gradualist strategy sowed the seeds for the structural problems with which China's economy struggles today.

5.1.1 Gradualism versus Shock Therapy

When the reforms were first adopted in China, a 'shock therapy' mirroring the rapid introduction of market forces by the Eastern European and former Soviet Union (EEFSU) economies was not desired, on account of the prevailing economic conditions. 'Gradualism' was preferred to more radical reform programmes. In 1978, the Chinese economy grew at a rate of 12.3 per cent; in other words, the socialist system appeared to be working well. There are always concerns over the measurement of growth and other statistics in the pre-reform and during the reform period. Suffice it to say that the economic situation in 1978 was not dire; thus, the impetus for a more radical type of reform was not present.

In contrast, the EEFSU societies in the late 1980s accepted a 'shock therapy' package, again under terms particular to their circumstances (notably, the lack of authority of the central government). Gradualism had been tried before the 1989 revolution without great success. One interpretation posited is that the ability to adopt gradualism or radical change depends on the extent to which the economy had stagnated and declined at the time of reform. The lower the growth potential of the old system, the stronger are the incentives and the will to pursue radical reform.

Gradualism is further related to initial conditions and economic structures. It is more likely to be successful in an underdeveloped and underindustrialized economy with a large surplus rural labour force. Rural incomes had been falling compared to urban incomes in China. The pre-existence of a declining sector, such as agriculture, results in a population of people who possess a strong demand for opportunities and who will also constitute a new labour force.

Thus, there are two main conditions that permit an incrementalist reform approach to be successful. First, China started its reforms before the state sector was in drastic decline, so that heavy subsidies were not needed, contrary to the situation of former Soviet firms in the late 1980s. Second, the start of rural reform and accompanying liberalization of private economic activity in the presence of a large rural labour surplus generated growth rapid enough to outpace the speed at which subsidies to SOEs were increasing. Another favourable condition is the political continuity of the government and its ability to control the process of growth. Murphy et al. (1992) show that the government's ability to impose and maintain quantity ceilings for goods and services sold at 'market prices' differentiates the success of China and the lack of success of the former Soviet Union.

Some of the changes under a gradualist approach were due less to planning, but are more accurately characterized as adjustment to practical circumstances. For example, one of the key steps in starting the reform process was the advent of 'household contract responsibility', that is, more and more farming households being entrusted with production and management under long-term contracts. This system, which was banned in 1979 but accepted when it became widely practised by rural residents, released rural productive forces and turned out to be the breakthrough of the rural reforms. This pattern was repeated when the rural economy was liberalized, with the rise of the township and village enterprises (TVEs), which were to become the dynamic engine of growth in the 1980s.

5.1.2 Regional Experimentation

Much of the innovation and many of the advances that occurred in the process of reform were less by design and resulted more from the Chinese government's pragmatic flexibility. The Chinese government approach can be described as 'no encouragement, no ban' (Naughton 1995). Experiments encompassing different reform programmes at various governmental levels were encouraged, including the creation of 'special economic zones', that is, specially designated areas in which export-oriented companies were permitted to flourish and become foreign-invested in these restricted locales, such as Shenzhen. Special treatment was further given to different regions, and local initiatives were respected.

This success has been attributed to particular forms of coordination (see Qian and Xu 1993). 'M-form' structures of coordination are based on minimal interdependence among regions or industries, so that experimentation in one area of industry can be completed without its success or failure causing disruptions across the economy. 'U-form' organization is characterized as 'top-down' because of more interdependence and thus experimentation could affect the whole system. M-form is thought to be more conducive to experimentation and heterogeneity among units than U-form hierarchies. China was perhaps leaning toward M-form coordination as a result of much decentralization that preceded the reform period, which accounts for the success of experiments in heralding further reforms.

5.1.3 The Theory of Partial Reform

Thus, a process characterized by partial reform was adopted in which some markets were liberalized and permitted to sell output at market prices, while being required to sell to state firms at administered prices. This dual-track system was extended to cover almost all economic transactions, except for credit markets where interest rates remain tightly controlled although a black market thrives in parallel; its own dual track, in a sense. Although the reforms were not accompanied by privatization of ownership, the resulting arrangements generated new forms of economic organizations. The most important is the creation of a parallel non-state sector. Much of China's dynamic growth can be attributed to the non-state sector, consisting of private and semi-private enterprises, including community-owned rural industrial enterprises, foreign joint ventures and individual businesses. The appeal of this approach in part stems from the fact that it honours 'implicit contracts', meeting expectations built up under a socialist system. The implicit contract guarantees a worker a wage regardless of effort, and benefits such as health insurance, free housing, retirement pension and jobs for life (the 'iron rice bowl') and for offspring. This reduces market efficiency and instead reflects vested interests. The gain from the maintenance of such distorted incentives is that resistance to reform is reduced.

It is important to note that the success of this approach depends mainly on the success of the new track. If the growth rate of the new sector is higher than that of the old sector, then the old system will in the long run shrink as a proportion of the economy. If the old economy stops expanding and the new economy grows, the new economy will dominate.

For instance, market prices for food were nearly twice as high as official prices by 1992, one decade after the start of reform. When governmental controls were removed, convergence occurred and food sold at officially set prices accounted for less than 15 per cent of total consumption. Under these conditions, convergence did not cause a 'shock'. The situation was similar in the foreign exchange market, where the unification of the official exchange rate and the 'swap market exchange rate' occurred at the end of 1993 when the differential between the two rates was about 50 per cent. At that time, only 20 per cent of such transactions were still subject to the official exchange rate (Fan 1994). The 'rationed' component did not shrink in absolute size but in relative terms with respect to the 'new track'. Perhaps one of the lessons is that the challenge in gradual transition is not to speed up the pace of reform, but to ensure that the old track does not grow. The old track cannot be ignored, because it may prosper as a parasite on the new track.

5.1.4 'Easy to Hard' Reform Sequence

With decentralization of decision-making powers to local governments and increased autonomy given to enterprises, there were a number of problems generated by this reform strategy. The gradualist approach actually means that reform measures are sequenced from 'easy' to 'hard':

the easy problems are addressed first, the hard ones are left for later. A radical approach would do the opposite: the aim would be to maximize efficiency gains and minimize implementation costs. However, restructuring may be easier with the gradualist approach as it minimizes the political costs of reform. Different conditions could produce a different optimum sequence. Thus, the voices heralding China as a model of growth should be heard with caution. For China itself, its transition has left it with a set of structural problems that are both 'hard' and intricately related to the centrally planned economy. The close relationship among the state, state-owned enterprises and state-owned banks is responsible for the amount of non-performing loans in the banking sector; the partial reform of state-owned enterprises is associated with urban unemployment; state ownership of large 'national champions' has affected the competitiveness of the enterprise sector. Other structural problems also include the legacy of the 'urban bias' industrialization policy, which has created a sizeable rural–urban income gap, limited job mobility, and contributed toward the largest migration in human history from rural to urban areas. Finally, the continuing role of the state creates a tension in the institutional foundations of the economy, whereby property rights tend to remain unclear and the transaction costs of contracting tend to be high. These structural issues are compounded by the resultant growth model of China.

5.2   ECONOMIC GROWTH IN THE CONTEXT OF WTO ACCESSION

This section presents a simple analytical framework as a starting point for discussing the growth model of China. First, gains from increasing inputs, such as capital and labour, constitute extensive growth. Intensive growth, on the other hand, requires advances in productivity, generally associated with increases in the technology parameter of the economy's growth model (Yueh 2013). Both can be affected by globalization and integration with the global economy.

Adapting the economic theory to the Chinese economy in transition, I posit that it is plausible that the growth sequence for a gradualist path could be characterized by closed development until extensive growth is exhausted and then open economy growth will follow. As a gradualist path is characterized by 'easy to hard' sequencing of reforms, gains from better allocation of existing factors are expected to occur first, as they are easier to achieve than growth in real productivity. When gains from such growth are exhausted, then an economy will stagnate until it is able to achieve gains in productivity. The economy is thus largely closed in the first stages in a gradualist path, as government control is the key ingredient in implementing a system of partial reform. As economic conditions worsen and the inefficient state sector begins to destabilize the economy with rising unemployment, there will likely be a gradual opening of the economy to permit foreign direct investment (FDI), exploit global demand and, importantly, negotiate technology transfers. When China announced in 1997 a five-year plan of lay-offs from the inefficient state sector, the signs of the limits of extensive growth were becoming more apparent.

Indeed, extensive growth has largely characterized China's growth thus far. Studies show that China's growth is associated less with gains in real productivity over the reform period, and more with increases in factor accumulation (for example, see the evidence cited in Wang and Yao 2001). As an example, surplus labour in the agricultural sector was efficiently reallocated with the creation of TVEs to absorb rural employment. This is not to discount the improvements gained from introducing market-oriented incentives in the state sector. In a study of state-owned enterprises, Groves et al. (1995) find that the introduction of even limited market incentives improved the performance of managers. However, the bulk of the empirical evidence indicates that China's growth is more similar to the East Asian 'tigers' factor accumulation process, which is associated with only small increases in real productivity (see Chow 1994). Having estimated the production function for the Chinese economy, Chow (1994) discusses the contribution to national output from the various inputs. He finds that although capital accumulation played a role in the growth process, there were no real productivity gains over the period 1952–80. As extensive growth reaches its limits due to diminishing returns, limits of capacity, ceasing population growth and, especially for China, already high levels of labour market participation make it unlikely that there would be a spurt. Early growth based on extensive growth is predicted to lead to a dramatic slowdown, which has been seen in other socialist economies, such as the Soviet Union between 1950 and the 1970s.

For China, though, there may still be room for gains from resource and factor reallocation. Better utilization of inputs of labour and capital has resulted from the introduction of market-oriented incentives and there remains room for more such gains; there is still surplus labour in its industries and capital constraints that have stifled private investment in capital stock. However, technological advancements will remain essential.

Like many developing countries, China aims to adopt or imitate the technology of advanced economies through foreign investment and capital inflows. This process is well known in development and is termed 'catching up'. At low levels of growth, the rate of growth can thus be substantial. China appears to be targeting its strategy toward promoting investment in technology sectors, such as the Shanghai-Pudong science park. Its ability to develop these centres remains to be seen, but its ability to upgrade the technological components of its manufactured goods is already in evidence.

Finally, China has achieved growth with minimal legal institutions; in fact, without private property, and thus a notable lack of the property rights which are thought to underlie efficient markets. Yet, China has grown rather well. It is thought that informal arrangements, such as trust or social capital – *guanxi* in Chinese – facilitated the economic transactions instead. However, there are likely to be limits to the extent that informal institutions can govern complex transactions with remote shareholders. Thus, continued growth will require laws and regulations, especially when prompted by the context of WTO-related international economic laws and the regulations needed to safeguard financial actors (Yueh 2011).

5.3   GLOBALIZATION AND GROWTH

The key determinant in a dual-track transition as undertaken by China is the existence of a new sector that grows relatively faster than the state sector, and can generate transfers to the state sector. Joining the WTO and integration into the global economy creates a new sector which can provide a source of growth while reforms are undertaken in the old sector. Moreover, global integration includes the potential to adopt international economic laws and best practice, such that there can be a speeding up of the learning curve for improving China's legal and institutional system. In other words, there is the potential to 'catch up' on the side of legal reforms.

Manufactured goods account for more than 90 per cent of merchandise exports in China. China is the largest exporter of manufactured products in the developing world (Lall and Albaladejo 2004). The growth of its manufactured exports has been among the fastest achieved by developing countries, and they are not, contrary to popular perception, based only on low-cost labour. Its exports span a broad range of technologies and are diversifying and upgrading with rapidity. Indeed, China has overtaken the United States (US) to become the world's largest trader.

In addition, despite the lack of full capital account convertibility, by the mid-1990s China had become the second-largest host country for foreign direct investment after the US, and the largest one among developing countries (not including flows through Hong Kong). There is some dispute over the figure on account of 'round-tripping', whereby capital leaves China and returns to take advantage of foreign capital concessions.

What is certain is that China is already a strong international competitor in a large range of industrial products, led by simple labour-intensive manufactures, but quickly diversifying into complex, capital- and technology-intensive goods. Liberalization can also induce technological upgrading, and the accompanying improvement in the business climate will make China an even more attractive location for FDI, with potential positive spillovers on domestic firms' productivity (Yueh 2013). As for the reciprocal entry into the domestic market, China has reduced the number of products subject to non-tariff barriers (that is, quotas and licences) from an estimated 1200 or so in the early 1990s to approximately 200 post-WTO entry. The pace of tariff reform has also been rapid: following a significant tariff reform in 1997, rates dropped to less than 20 per cent across the board (Lardy 1998). Opening has given China a further source of growth while domestic consumption grows and as the government reins in investment and its own spending.

There are also indications of rapid legal reforms, which are increasingly aligning China with international economic and business standards. These include the adoption of mergers and acquisitions and bankruptcy legislation as well as international accounting standards. As international norms and national laws can be viewed as sources of best practice, there is the possibility for China to create an institutional system that draws on the experiences of other countries and can help it to leapfrog the process of building a legal and regulatory system. In many ways, global integration can help to resolve the structural problem seen in China's growth model whereby property rights can become defined by contract while the economy transforms into a more market-oriented one.

However, opening and globalization is not without its own set of risks. The pertinent lessons here can be drawn from the recent financial crises. Indeed, China's relative immunity from recent events has often been touted as one of the remarkable features of the Chinese path. This has been interpreted to suggest that China will continue to grow without reservation. I caution against such a view, as China's ability to weather the crisis is likely to have more to do with the stage of its gradualist path.

In brief, for China, the lack of comprehensive liberalization of trade and financial services may have insulated it from the destabilizing effects of the global economy. In addition, the lack of privatization, exchange rate controls, and limited credit available to non-state enterprises all contributed to relative insulation. The gradualist path predicted this outcome to some extent. However, China has not been immune from the global economy slowdown, and this is likely to become more characteristic as it becomes a more open economy. As China becomes more open and integrated into the global economy, and particularly as it is liberalizing its banking and financial sector as part of its WTO accession terms, it will be more susceptible to macroeconomic instability (Sachs and Woo 2003). The reform of the exchange rate will be an important factor in mitigating this risk. Yet, as the history of emerging markets suggests, the need to open and liberalize is not without substantial risk if not managed appropriately.

5.4 CONCLUSIONS

China has performed admirably well since market-oriented reforms were introduced in the late 1970s. I have analysed the nature of its development path and growth model, which have resulted in a set of structural issues in the Chinese economy yet to be resolved. Opening to the global economy provides a source of growth that can help to sustain the reforms needed to address the structural problems. However, opening raises its own set of challenges, particularly the risk of macroeconomic instability.

I conclude with a cautiously optimistic view of the sustainability of China's economic growth, based on some promising signs. There are significant amounts of household savings in China. Increasing consumer credit can stimulate aggregate demand in an economy with little household debt. Indeed, the government's fiscal stimulus policy package has been increasing public investment in infrastructure, especially in interior regions, for several years.

Finally, accession to WTO has opened foreign markets to Chinese goods and given it another source of growth via exports while it undertakes domestic reforms. International economic law has also given China a source of best practice with which to reform its legal system. Globalization alone would not resolve the structural problems in the Chinese economy, but it offers the government some room for tackling the continuing legacy issues in the industrial sector and the divisions between the urban and rural sectors of the economy.

In conclusion, China has been a remarkable economy in transition, without a doubt. Perhaps most importantly, in stark contrast to the standard of living achieved under the centrally planned economy, this growth is correlated with an improvement in the standard of living for the Chinese people. Whether it is sustainable and aided by globalization and integration into the world economy has been my query.

Given the 'easy to hard' sequence that characterizes China's reform strategy, there are many challenges that lie ahead. The coincidence of the 'hard' issues with an opening of the economy to global trade provides possible ways to grow within the constraints of a partial reform strategy. However, opening brings about a set of new concerns, including short-term macroeconomic instability and financial crises. The challenges of

China's continued development will test the ultimate success of a gradualist reform strategy in an economy increasingly open to global factors.

REFERENCES

Chow, G.C. (1994), *Understanding China's Economy*, Singapore: World Scientific Publishing.

Fan, G. (1994), 'Incremental Change and Dual-Tack Transition: Understanding the Case of China', *Economic Policy* 19(Supp.), 99–122.

Groves, T., H. Yongmiao, J. McMillan and B. Naughton (1995), 'China's Evolving Managerial Market', *Journal of Political Economy* 103(4), 873–92.

Lall, S. and M. Albaladejo (2004), 'The Competitive Impact of China on Manufactured Exports by Emerging Economies in Asia', *World Development* 32(9), 1441–66.

Lardy, N.R. (1998), *China's Unfinished Economic Revolution*, Washington, DC: Brookings Institution.

Murphy, K.M., A. Schleifer and R.W. Vishny (1992), 'The Transition to a Market Economy: Pitfalls of Partial Reform', *Quarterly Journal of Economics* 107(3), 889–906.

Naughton, B. (1995), *Growing out of the Plan*, Cambridge: Cambridge University Press.

Qian, Y. and C. Xu (1993), 'The M-form Hierarchy and China's Economic Reform', *European Economic Review* 37, 541–8.

Riskin, C. (1987), *China's Political Economy*, Oxford: Oxford University Press.

Sachs, J. and W.T. Woo (2003), 'China's Growth after WTO Membership', *Journal of Chinese Economics and Business Studies* 1(1), 1–31.

Wang, Y. and Y. Yao (2003), 'Sources of China's Economic Growth: 1952–99: Incorporating Human Capital Accumulation', *China Economic Review* 14(1), 32–52.

Yueh, L. (2011), *Enterprising China: Business, Economic, and Legal Development Since 1979*, Oxford: Oxford University Press.

Yueh, L. (2012), *The Economy of China*, Cheltenham, UK and Northampton, MA, USA: Edward Elgar Publishing.

Yueh, L. (2013), *China's Growth: The Making of an Economic Superpower*, Oxford: Oxford University Press.

6. Non-price components of market share gains: evidence for EU countries

Konstantīns Beņkovskis and Julia Wörz

Competitiveness has many dimensions and therefore many different measures are traditionally used to assess the competitiveness of countries. The choice of measurement varies depending on whether the focus lies on the firm, the industry, the country or the regional level.[1] At the country level, which is most relevant for economic policy, two approaches can be distinguished: the broad definition and the narrow definition. The broad definition compares macroeconomic performance and overall living standards across countries and focuses on productivity measures. The productivity level of an economy depends on the efficiency of production and the value of the output produced. According to Porter et al. (2007) a wide range of determinants work together to establish a country's overall competitiveness: endowments, including natural resources, geographic location, historical legacy and the like; the macroeconomic, political, legal and social context given by the country's policies and institutions; and microeconomic competitiveness given by the business environment, linkages and externalities between the firms operating in the country and their sophistication. The European Commission adopts such a broad definition in its annual European Competitiveness Report. The latest edition focuses in particular in microeconomic aspects of competitiveness (European Commission 2015). The narrow definition focuses on a country's ability to sell its products on the world market and focuses on price and cost measures. This definition of competitiveness in international trade is adopted for example by the Organisation for Economic Co-operation and Development (OECD) (see https://stats.oecd.org/glossary/detail.asp?ID=399).

In addition, private institutions such as the World Economic Forum or the Heritage Foundation have constructed comprehensive indices of competitiveness (http://reports.weforum.org/global-competitiveness-report-2015-2016/competitiveness-rankings/, and http://www.heritage.org/index/about). Even though these indices incorporate a broad range of indicators, which cover various aspects of an economy, they tend to narrow the focus down to a simple one-dimensional ranking of countries, as the underlying dimensions of the index are often not reported as prominently as the country list of best performers. Very much in contrast to this 'simplifying' ranking of economies, the research network on competitiveness (CompNet) established by the European Central Bank (ECB) provides a long and diverse list of traditional and newly developed indicators, which should give a comprehensive and differentiated overview of the competitive performance of individual countries (Karadeloglou et al. 2015). This, however, entails the great challenge that communicating the results is a difficult task.

The attractiveness of the narrow definition, focusing on very specific trade outcomes such as market shares, or on specific price and cost measures such as the real effective exchange rate, lies in the ease of calculation and communication as these measures are generally well understood by the public and by economic policy makers. This makes this definition rather attractive and explains the strong use of price and cost measures as competitiveness indicators. Yet, a too-narrow focus on such indicators can yield vastly misleading results, as is illustrated in Figure 6.1. It is common knowledge that a real appreciation makes a country's exports more expensive and should hence result in a falling global market share. Figure 6.1 shows indeed that for some countries a real appreciation goes hand in hand with a decline in global market share. These are in particular some core euro area countries and most cohesion countries in the European Union (EU). However, for the Central, Eastern and South-Eastern European (CESEE) EU member states we witness a contrasting trade outcome: their market share has risen over the period 1995 to 2011[2] despite a substantial real appreciation of their currencies. Clearly, appreciation was a consequence of successful catching-up and not an indication of worsened price competitiveness in this case.

In this chapter, we offer a simple and well-understood indicator of competitiveness – changes in global market shares – but we decompose this indicator into various contributions arising from price and cost measures, other non-price factors (including changes in product quality and consumers' tastes), and structural factors such as shifts in global demand patterns, entry and exit of competitors, and so on. A special and rather new factor is the increased international fragmentation of production. Newly available data allow us to also gauge the effect of a country's integration in global production networks on its competitiveness as measured by changes in its global market shares. Hence, our decomposition reflects different dimensions underlying a country's competitiveness. Knowing more about underlying factors behind market share changes is crucial in order to draw policy-relevant conclusions.

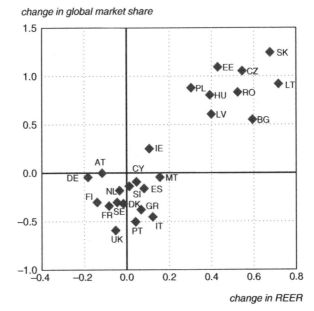

Notes: REER = real effective exchange rate. AT = Austria. BG = Bulgaria. CY = Cyprus.
CZ = Czech Republic. DE = Germany. DK = Denmark. EE = Estonia. ES = Spain.
FI = Finland. FR = France. GR = Greece. HU = Hungary. IE = Ireland. IT = Italy.
LT = Lithuania. LV = Latvia. MT = Malta. NL = Netherlands. PL = Poland.
PT = Portugal. RO = Romania. SE= Sweden. SI = Slovenia. SK = Slovakia.
UK = United Kingdom.

Sources: Eurostat, Comtrade (United Nations), authors' calculations.

*Figure 6.1   Cumulative changes in market shares and real effective
            exchange rates of EU member states, 1995–2011*

We present our measure of market share changes, its decomposition and
the necessary data sources in Section 6.1, Section 6.2 reports the results
based on gross exports, Section 6.3 refines these findings when we focus on
a country's value added in exports rather than on traditional gross trade
data, which are plagued by the double counting of trade in intermediate
goods. Section 6.4 concludes.

6.1   METHOD AND DATA SOURCES

Our aim is to capture the multidimensional property of competitiveness
as well as its relative nature, while keeping the results tractable and clear.

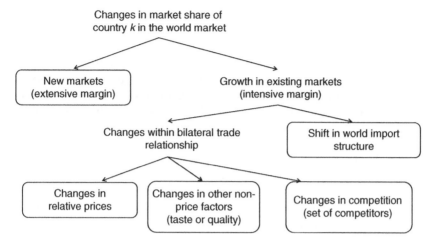

Figure 6.2   Schematic representation of market share decomposition

Therefore we propose to use the change in global market share as a simple and comprehensive measure of competitiveness. Since this outcome-based measure alone does not lead to policy-relevant conclusions, we decompose the change in global market shares into various input factors. This decomposition is theoretically derived from the consumer utility maximization problem.[3] The details of the decomposition are given in Benkovskis and Wörz (2015). Figure 6.2 shows the main elements of this decomposition. First, we distinguish between the growth in market shares that arises from entering entirely new markets (reflecting the so-called extensive margin of trade growth), whereby a market is defined at the product-destination level, and growth in existing markets (the so-called intensive margin). Second, we distinguish between changes in bilateral trade relationships and market share changes that arise from changes in global demand patterns. Market shares of a specific exporter are affected if the demand coming from specific regions rises or falls. Finally, we decompose the bilateral trade flows of a specific exporter into the changes in prices and costs of the exporter, changes in the set of competitors (as the entry of new exporters in the same market automatically diminishes export shares of incumbent exporters) and a residual which – following from the theoretical foundation of the decomposition – can be interpreted as changes in non-price factors such as the relative quality of export products or consumers' valuation of these products. We arrive at five distinct components: diversification into new markets, shifts in world import structure, changes in relative prices, changes in non-price factors (interpreted as quality and taste), and entry and exit of competitors.

This decomposition is based on data for gross exports of final use products. Hence, it can lead to potentially biased results due to international fragmentation of production. Consider a country that increasingly specializes in the assembly of high-quality export goods (such as cars or electronics) whereby the high-quality components are imported intermediates. In our decomposition we would find a rising positive contribution of non-price factors (relative quality of the export goods) for this country. Yet, such an interpretation would be highly misleading since the quality components are mostly imported.

Therefore, in a second step we refine our decomposition in the following way: rather than basing the calculations on gross export flows, we focus on the value added of each exporter in each export good worldwide. This can be done by combining information on global trade flows with information on international input–output linkages. Rather than decomposing gross exports of final use products, we decompose the domestic value added in exports of each country. In this second decomposition we further obtain an additional term which captures the impact of shifts in global production networks. For example, a country's value-added export market share can increase due to a higher domestic content in its exports or due to its stronger involvement in international production networks.

The empirical application is based on highly disaggregated trade data and global input–output data over the period 1995–2011. We obtain the former from the United Nations (UN) Comtrade database. From this database we extract bilateral import values and quantities for all importers and exporters at the Harmonized System (HS) six-digit level. For the decomposition of value added in exports, we also use information from the World Input–Output Database (WIOD), which contains the international input–output linkages for 40 exporting countries (including all EU members) and 59 products according to the Statistical Classification of Products by Activity (CPA). Unfortunately there is no update of the WIOD data available, hence we are unable to calculate the decomposition of domestic value added in exports for more recent years than 2011. In the analysis we focus on the exports of 25 EU members (excluding Belgium, Luxembourg and Croatia for data reasons) and on final products only. The latter limitation is necessary in order to obtain comparable results between the traditional view based on gross exports and the value-added view.

6.2   MARKET SHARE CHANGES OF EU MEMBER STATES IN THE TRADITIONAL VIEW

A simple calculation of cumulative market share changes based on gross exports (see Figure 6.3) reveals that a subset of EU member states

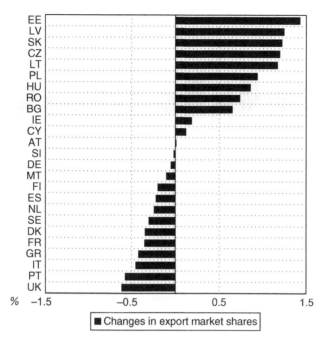

Figure 6.3   Cumulative changes in global market shares, 1996–2011

has gained global market shares over the period 1996–2011, reflecting an improvement in their international competitiveness. This subset of countries consists with only one exception of the CESEE countries that joined the EU in 2004 and 2007. In addition, Ireland shows a clear gain in traditional export shares. Slovenia experienced a marginal loss in its global market share, but can safely be classified as one of four EU member states that *grosso modo* maintained their world market shares, together with Cyprus, Germany and Austria. Given the increasing importance of large global traders such as China and other emerging economies over this period, this performance can also be seen as a success. All remaining EU member states lost world market shares, in particular so the Southern European countries and the United Kingdom (UK).

These changes in global market shares may be due to factors that are

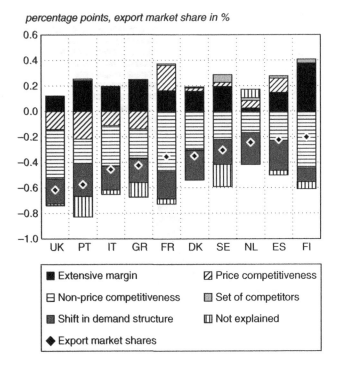

percentage points, export market share in %

Note: DK = Denmark. ES = Spain. FI = Finland. FR = France. GR = Greece. IT = Italy. NL = Netherlands. PT = Portugal. SE = Sweden. UK = United Kingdom.

Figure 6.4   Decomposition of traditional export market share losses, 1996–2011

largely outside the control of local policy-makers – for instance, the entry of new competitors automatically reduces market shares of all incumbent exporters holding all other factors constant – or may be easily influenced by domestic policies. Our decomposition of market share changes sheds some light on the nature of different factors underlying market share changes. Figures 6.4 and 6.5 illustrate the results of our decomposition analysis for those EU members that experienced notable changes in their global market share. Figure 6.4 summarizes the countries that experienced market share losses. Rather uniformly, all countries show a negative contribution of non-price factors, suggesting that the quality of their exports or consumers' valuation of their export goods has deteriorated relative to their competitors between 1996 and 2011. Further, changes in global demand structures have been unfavourable for those Western and Northern EU member states. The results for price competitiveness are

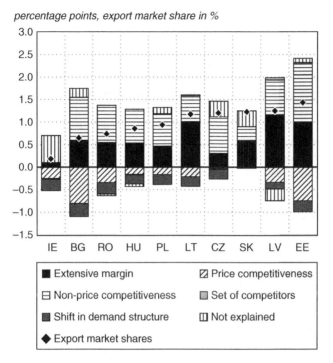

percentage points, export market share in %

Note: BG = Bulgaria. CZ = Czech Republic. EE = Estonia. HU = Hungary. IE = Ireland. LT = Lithuania. LV = Latvia. PL = Poland. RO = Romania. SK = Slovakia.

Figure 6.5   Decomposition of traditional export market share gains, 1996–2011

more mixed. While France, Spain, the Netherlands, Sweden and Denmark show a positive contribution from price competitiveness, Portugal, Greece, the UK and Italy exhibit a clear deterioration in price competitiveness according to our calculations. Finally, for all countries market share losses would have been even larger had they not at the same time diversified into new markets (defined here at the product and destination level). In other words the extensive margin of trade showed a positive contribution to changes in market shares over this period.[4]

Figure 6.5 contains the results for the CESEE EU members that could widen their global market share, and for Ireland. Again, the extensive margin of trade – or exploration of new product-destination markets – supported market share gains. The contribution is notably strong for the CESEE countries, reflecting their larger potential for diversification as they are catching-up economies. In contrast to the results for the Western and Northern European countries, non-price competitiveness shows a positive and large contribution in this subset of countries, suggesting that the relative quality of CESEE exports has improved substantially between 1996 and 2011.[5] Further, all countries in Figure 6.5 exhibit a deterioration in their price competitiveness, with the exception of Slovakia where this component yields a zero contribution. The gain in market shares despite worsening price competitiveness is reconcilable with the catching-up performance of these countries. Like the market share losers, the winners did not manage to respond adequately to changes in global demand patterns; the contribution of this factor is negative for all CESEE countries (albeit very small in Slovakia) and for Ireland.

6.3   CHANGES IN VALUE-ADDED MARKET SHARES

Before we turn to the decomposition of value-added market shares, let us compare the absolute changes in value added to gross export market shares. Not surprisingly the differences are rather small, as shown in Figure 6.6, as at the global level, value-added and export market shares should be equal. Basically, observed differences arise from the differential value-added composition of gross exports and final use products. We observe that the strongly internationally integrated CESEE countries often show slightly smaller market share gains in value-added terms, while the losses in market shares are also smaller for countries such as Greece, Portugal and the UK. Yet, the broad picture does not change. Core and southern periphery countries lose market shares, while catching-up CESEE countries and Ireland gain world market shares.

However, the underlying story concerning the components changes considerably. The components of changes in market share in some cases appear radically different when analysing gross export versus value added in exports. The most important difference is that price competitiveness has improved for almost all countries when adopting the value-added view in contrast to the mixed contribution to gross exports (see Figures 6.7 and 6.8). We further observe a negative contribution to market share growth from integration into global production networks in most countries in Figure 6.7. This could mean that the rising degree of outsourcing has exerted a downward pressure on market shares for these countries. Only Portugal and Greece show a positive contribution from stronger integration in global production networks. These countries are likely to be the recipients of activities that are outsourced in the process of further economic integration. As before, the contribution of entering new markets

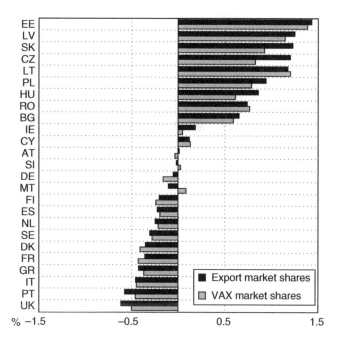

Note: VAX market shares = value-added market shares. AT = Austria. BE = Belgium. BG = Bulgaria. CY = Cyprus. CZ = Czech Republic. DE = Germany. DK = Denmark. EE = Estonia. ES = Spain. FI = Finland. FR = France. GR = Greece. HR = Croatia. HU = Hungary. IE = Ireland. IT = Italy. LT = Lithuania. LU = Luxembourg. LV = Latvia. MT = Malta. NL = Netherlands. PL = Poland. PT = Portugal. RO = Romania. SE = Sweden. SK = Slovakia. SI = Slovenia. UK = United Kingdom.

Figure 6.6   Cumulative changes in export and value-added global market shares, 1996–2011

is small but positive, while the contribution of shifts in global demand is negative for all countries.

More striking differences are observed for the subset of market share winners (see Figure 6.8). In sharp contrast to the traditional analysis based on gross exports, we do not observe losses in price competitiveness, with the exception of Bulgaria, Estonia and Ireland. In the latter case, the contribution is roughly neutral. In all other countries, we again observe a rise in price competitiveness. At the same time, the apparent gains in non-price competitiveness are not sustained in this view. When we trace only the share of domestic value added of each country in world exports, we find a negative contribution of non-price factors. This reflects their position in global value chains as assembly locations. Put differently, these countries would have experienced even stronger gains in global market shares

percentage points, export market share in %

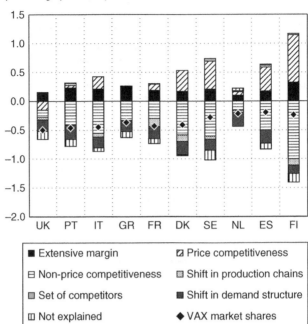

Note: VAX market shares = valued-added market shares. DK = Denmark. ES = Spain.
FI = Finland. FR = France. GR = Greece. IT = Italy. NL = Netherlands. PT = Portugal.
SE = Sweden. UK = United Kingdom.

Figure 6.7   Decomposition of value-added market share losses, 1996–2011

had they also increased the relative quality and valuation of the domestic
content of their export goods, or moved into higher value-added parts
of the production chain. Finally, the contribution of the integration into
global production networks is now mostly positive (the only exception is
Ireland). As before, the positive contribution of entry into new markets
is stronger than for the Western and Northern EU countries. Further,
changes in global demand patterns exert a drag on market share growth.

6.4   CONCLUSIONS

Our decomposition of changes in markets shares into price factors, non-
price factors, net gains from entering new markets, net pressure from

percentage points, export market share in %

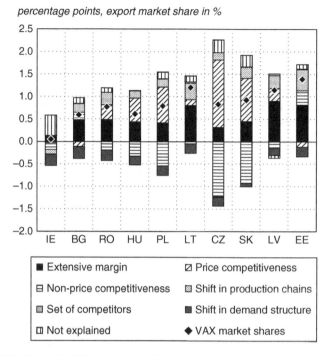

Note: BG = Bulgaria. CZ = Czech Republic. EE = Estonia. HU = Hungary. IE = Ireland. LT = Lithuania. LV = Latvia. PL = Poland. RO = Romania. SK = Slovakia.

Figure 6.8   Decomposition of value-added market share gains, 1996–2011

additional competitors, shifts in global demand and the effects of integration into global production networks for EU member states over the period 1996–2011 revealed a clear differentiation between Eastern and Western European countries. While the former gained global market shares, the latter lost importance as exporters. Only a few countries – Germany, Austria, Slovenia and Cyprus – could maintain their global market share. In the face of strongly rising shares by emerging economies such as China, the ability to maintain global market shares can well be seen as a successful development.

These aggregated trade outcomes remain unaffected whether we focus attention on gross exports – including imported intermediates – or domestic value added in global exports. However, the decomposition of market share gains or losses tells a rather different story depending on which view is adopted. In our view, the focus should be on domestic value added as this is relevant for overall living standards and welfare.

Adopting this view we find that the vast majority of EU member states show improvements in price competitiveness over the period. This is in contrast to the gross export view where especially the CESEE countries display losses in price competitiveness. These differences between both views also suggest that the increasing fragmentation of production and economic integration supports an efficient allocation of resources, hence leading to improvements in price competitiveness for the EU members. However, the integration into global production networks seems to be beneficial mostly for the catching-up economies (Southern and Eastern EU countries) and undermines the competitiveness of more advanced economies. As such, integration appears to foster convergence. We further observe that apparent improvements in CESEE non-price competitiveness based on gross exports arise largely from relocating production stages into those countries. In other words, the closing of the quality gap arises not least from relocating production stages into those countries which allow them to process higher-quality inputs into higher-quality export goods, while the domestic value added in the production of these goods does not show similar improvements in non-price factors.

Finally, we observe two features that are independent of the view chosen: first, all EU member states have profited from diversifying into new markets. This positive contribution is, unsurprisingly, much more important for the Eastern and Southern catching-up economies. Hence the question arises how these countries prepare for the time when this catching-up related window of opportunity closes. Second, all EU member states failed to adapt swiftly to changing global demand patterns. This yields implications for industrial policies to adopt a more forward-looking view and to identify future demand patterns early on.

NOTES

1. For a discussion on the definition of competitiveness see, for example, Krugman (1994) and Landesmann and Wörz (2006).
2. For reasons of data availability and in order to ensure comparability throughout this chapter we base our analysis on the period 1995–2011.
3. A country's global export market share is interpreted as the sum of its import shares by all other countries. Consumers in importing countries can choose between domestic and imported products, whereby imports are imported from different source countries (representing different varieties), and we allow for changes in varieties, the imported product set, and the taste for and quality of those imports.
4. Note that we look at the cumulative change here; this explains the rather high contribution of the extensive margin.
5. Note that relative changes in quality and taste are measured here and not absolute levels of quality.

REFERENCES

Beņkovskis, K. and J. Wörz (2015), '"Made in China" – How Does it Affect Measures of Competitiveness?', European Central Bank Working Paper 1787, April.

European Commission (ed.) (2015), 'European Competitiveness Report 2014: Helping Firms Grow', Commission Staff Working Document SWD(2014)277. http://ec.europa.eu/growth/industry/competitiveness/reports/eu-competitive ness-report/index_en.htm.

Karadeloglou, P. and K. Beņkovskis (eds) and CompNet Task Force (2015), 'Compendium on the Diagnostic Toolkit for Competitiveness', European Central Bank Occasional Paper 163, July.

Krugman, P. (1994), 'Competitiveness: A Dangerous Obsession', *Foreign Affairs* 73(2), 28–44.

Landesmann, M. and J. Wörz (2006), 'CEECs' Competitiveness in the Global Context', wiiw Research Report 327, Vienna Institute for International Economic Studies.

Porter, M.E., C. Ketels, M. Delgado and R. Bryden (2007), 'Competitiveness at the Crossroads: Choosing the Future Direction of the Russian Economy', Moscow: Center for Strategic Research.

PART III

EU structural policies

7. EU economic governance: euro area periphery lessons for Central and Eastern European countries*

Zsolt Darvas

Before the crisis that evolved in 2008 and during its aftermath, there were many similarities between the macroeconomic developments of euro area periphery and Central and Eastern European (CEE) EU member states. Before the crisis, almost all countries in both regions experienced rapid economic growth, which to a large extent was fuelled by capital inflows (Figure 7.1). Capital inflows resulted in macroeconomic imbalances, such as too-fast domestic credit growth, large current account deficits and the accumulation of large foreign liabilities (Darvas and Szapáry 2010).[1]

There were also a number of similarities between the two regions during the global and euro area crises and their aftermath. A notable development was the switch from large current account deficits to surpluses, which were related to a slowdown or even reversal of private capital flows, partly fuelled by the deleveraging of foreign-owned banks. During 2009–10, the initial adjustment was more gradual in the euro area periphery due to European Central Bank (ECB) liquidity provision to banks, and starting from 2010, European Union (EU) and International Monetary Fund (IMF) financial assistance to Greece, Ireland, Portugal and Spain. These official inflows allowed a smoother adjustment on the external position than that which occurred in most CEE countries, especially in the Baltics. CEE countries did not benefit from the support of the ECB (Darvas 2009),[2] while official flows in the framework of the financial assistance to Hungary, Latvia and Romania were small compared to the receding private capital flows. Yet capital flow trends remained broadly similar in both country groups (Figure 7.1).

Notwithstanding the similarities, there were and are important differences between euro area periphery and Central and Eastern European

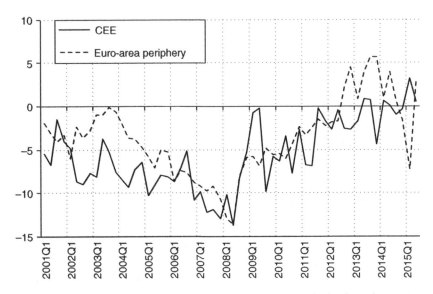

Note: Euro area periphery includes Greece, Ireland, Portugal and Spain. Central European (CEE) countries include Bulgaria, Czech Republic, Croatia, Estonia, Hungary, Latvia, Lithuania, Poland, Romania, Slovenia. A negative value indicates capital inflows.

Source: Eurostat, International Monetary Fund and Bruegel calculations.

Figure 7.1   Net financial account of the euro periphery and Central and Eastern European EU countries (% of GDP)

member states. Foreign direct investment (FDI), which is a more stable form of capital flows, accounted for about half of capital inflows to CEE countries, while it was negligible in euro area periphery countries. Euro area periphery countries inherited from the pre-crisis period the misalignment of wages and productivity, accumulated large foreign debt, large public debts, little integration into global value chains, a large share of small and medium-sized enterprises, and weak institutional quality. Few of these weaknesses characterize CEE countries, which are therefore in better shape than the euro area periphery countries to cope with post-crisis economic challenges. The purpose of this chapter is to discuss the role of EU economic governance in pre- and post-crisis macroeconomic developments of euro area periphery countries and to draw lessons for the CEE region.

7.1 EU GOVERNANCE FRAMEWORKS FOR STRUCTURAL REFORMS

7.1.1 The Pre-Crisis Framework

The pre-crisis belief among European policymakers was that fiscal discipline and price stability are sufficient for smart, sustainable and inclusive growth. Large capital flows were assessed as a benign phenomenon, reflecting increased economic integration between European countries. Certainly, capital inflows and the consequent current account deficits and surpluses are not necessarily a bad thing. They may reflect the improved utilization of resources when capital moves to fast-growing regions to the benefit of both the source and the recipient countries. However, the booms and busts in the Irish and Spanish housing sectors exemplify capital misallocation (Ahearne et al. 2008). Additionally, the accumulation of 'excessive' debt in a country (or a region of a monetary union) is undesirable. There are good reasons to conclude that the external debt of Greece, Portugal and Spain became excessive (Darvas 2012). Excessive capital inflows can also lead to distortions in the wage formation process, whereby labour demand resulting from the capital inflow-induced housing booms pushes up wage growth over the growth rate of productivity.

Given the belief in fiscal discipline and price stability, there were no effective European instruments to support national structural policies in avoiding unsustainable macroeconomic developments. There was some economic policy coordination in the EU under the so-called 'broad economic policy guidelines' and the staff of the European Commission occasionally prepared reports (usually of extensive length, with several hundred pages), which highlighted that some developments may lead to vulnerabilities. But there were no proper mechanisms to foster structural adjustment. Structural adjustment has two main and interrelated aspects: a microeconomic dimension, such as regulations and policies that affect the business climate, the flexibility of markets, banking activities, innovation and the educational system of the country, and so on; and a macroeconomic dimension, which is primarily reflected in aggregate productivity changes, price and wage competitiveness, and external balances.

Still, some countries were able to adjust within the euro area without a European-level involvement. For example, Germany's price and wage competitiveness improved significantly from the mid-1990s until the onset of the crisis, while its current account deficit turned to a sizeable surplus (Darvas 2015).[3] But others, such as Greece, Italy, Spain and Portugal, were not able to adjust. While Germany, Italy and Portugal had the worst growth performances among euro area member states before the crisis,

Germany boosted its competitiveness during this period, but Italy and Portugal did not. Booming domestic demand contributed to rapid economic growth in Spain and Greece before the crisis, which obscured the more serious structural problems.

It is therefore safe to conclude that the pre-crisis economic governance framework of the EU was insufficient, as it neglected micro- and macroeconomic aspects of structural adjustment, and as euro area periphery countries entered the global financial and economic crisis with highly vulnerable positions. The accumulated problems of these countries left difficult choices during the crisis. Given their euro area membership, a currency depreciation (which would have helped to address macroeconomic imbalance problems) was not an option.[4] What remained were the so-called 'internal devaluation' (decrease in wages and prices relative to trading partners), fiscal adjustment and structural reforms (institutions, public sector, insolvency frameworks, red tape, product and labour markets, education, social redistribution, and so on). All three policy areas included measures which aggravated the recession that these countries entered, and increased social pain.

7.1.2 The Revamped EU Framework for Structural Policies

The EU's framework for structural policies has been revamped significantly during the crisis. A new yearly cycle of economic policy coordination, called the European Semester, was inaugurated in 2011. It starts with the setting of the main priorities by the European Commission in an Annual Growth Survey, followed by the submission and assessment of EU member state National Reform Programmes and Stability and Convergence Programmes. It concludes with country-specific recommendations, and recommendations for the euro area as a whole.

A new procedure, the so-called Macroeconomic Imbalance Procedure (MIP), has been introduced with the aim of preventing and correcting private sector imbalances, such as weak competitiveness positions and high private debt.[5] Whenever a country has a really excessive imbalance, the so-called Excessive Imbalance Procedure is activated (this has not yet happened to any EU country). The EIP has similarities to the Excessive Deficit Procedure under the EU's Stability and Growth Pact.

In my view, the Macroeconomic Imbalance Procedure is a major innovation in the EU's economic governance framework, because the neglect of private sector vulnerabilities was a major reason behind the depth and the length of the euro area crisis. However, in Darvas and Vihriälä (2013) and Darvas and Leandro (2015) we concluded that the European Semester, including the Macroeconomic Imbalance Procedure, is rather ineffective.

One aspect of our assessment is based on the implementation of the country-specific recommendations made under the European Semester. Recommendations made in the context of an Excessive Deficit Procedure (EDP) and an Excessive Imbalance Procedure (EIP) are binding. For other recommendations, member states 'shall take due account of the guidance addressed to them in the development of their economic, employment and budgetary policies before taking key decisions on their national budgets for the succeeding years'.[6] Non-compliance with recommendations can lead to warnings, further recommendations and enhanced monitoring, and in the case of EDP and EIP requirements, non-compliance can even lead to financial sanctions.

In Darvas and Leandro (2015) we create a 'European Semester reform implementation index', which is a numerical quantification of the European Commission's assessment of the implementation of recommendations (see details in the notes to Figure 7.2). Figure 7.2 shows that implementation of

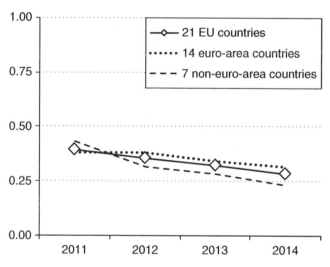

Note: We gave a score of 1 to 'full/substantial progress', a score of 0.5 to 'some progress' and a score of 0 to 'no/limited progress': our indicator is the ratio of the sum of the scores to the total number of recommendations. Progress assessments are primarily based on European Commission assessments. We report an unweighted average of those 21 EU countries for which data are available for all years: Austria, Belgium, Bulgaria, Czech Republic, Denmark, Estonia, Finland, France, Germany, Hungary, Italy, Lithuania, Luxembourg, Malta, Netherlands, Poland, Slovakia, Slovenia, Spain, Sweden and the United Kingdom. The horizontal axis indicates the date of the European Semester recommendations.

Source: Darvas and Leandro (2015).

Figure 7.2   European Semester reform implementation index

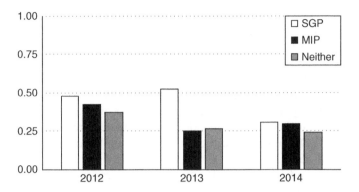

N

Notes: See the notes to Figure 7.2 for the method of calculation. Some recommendations are related for both the SGP and MIP, which are taken into account for both procedures. SGP = Stability and Growth Pact. MIP = Macroeconomic Imbalance Procedure.

Source: Darvas and Leandro (2015).

Figure 7.3 *European Semester implementation rates according to the type of recommendations*

recommendations given under the European Semester was modest (40 per cent in the EU according to our indicator) at its inception in 2011. In spite of the efforts made to improve the European Semester in recent years the implementation index fell steadily to 29 per cent by 2014.

As Figure 7.3 shows, the rate of implementation of recommendations related to the Stability and Growth Pact (SGP) is typically higher (44 per cent on average in 2012–14) than the implementation of recommendations related to the Macroeconomic Imbalance Procedure (32 per cent in 2012–14) and other recommendations (29 per cent in 2012–14). Even though SGP recommendations have the strongest legal basis, the average 44 per cent implementation rate cannot be regarded as large. The EIP implementation rate is even lower, suggesting that the European Semester is not particularly effective in enforcing the EU's fiscal and macroeconomic imbalance rules.

Furthermore, it is striking that the rate of implementation of European Semester recommendations (which are based on huge efforts by European institutions to coordinate economic policies in the EU) is not higher than the rate of implementation of the Organisation for Economic Co-operation and Development's (OECD) unilateral recommendations, as Figure 7.4 reports. Overlaps between the European Semester and OECD recommendations only partly explain this similarity.

I therefore conclude that the European economic governance framework

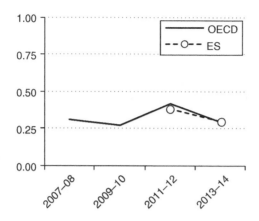

Notes: See the notes to Figure 7.2 on the European Semester reform implementation index. For the OECD Going for Growth recommendations, we report the 'Overall reform responsiveness rate', which is calculated by the OECD. Unweighted average for those 16 EU countries for which data is available in the full period: Austria, Belgium, Czech Republic, Denmark, Finland, France, Germany, Hungary, Italy, Luxembourg, Netherlands, Poland, Slovakia, Spain, Sweden and the United Kingdom. OECD = Organisation for Economic Co-operation and Development. ES = European Semester.

Source: Darvas and Leandro (2015) and OECD data.

Figure 7.4   Reform implementation: comparison of European Semester and OECD Going for Growth recommendations

is not effective in fostering structural reforms. Instead, reform is fostered by other factors. A simple visual check of the European Semester implementation rate and the OECD reform responsiveness rate suggests that the countries under a financial assistance programme or undergoing severe macroeconomic adjustments implement the most. The highest reform responsiveness rate, 92 per cent, was observed in Greece in 2011–12 according to the OECD. In the same period, the reform responsiveness rate was 82 per cent for Ireland and 77 per cent for Portugal. Estonia, a country undergoing severe macroeconomic adjustment, had a high score too (80 per cent). Next in the ranking is Spain with a reform responsiveness rate of 70 per cent. The only other occasion with a similarly high reform responsiveness rate was for Hungary in 2007–08 (73 per cent), when Hungary had already started a major fiscal and macroeconomic adjustment process. In all of these countries, the reform responsiveness rate fell in the next time period (though it typically remained above the EU average), when either the financial assistance programme ended (Ireland and Portugal), or market pressure eased (Hungary and Spain), or reform fatigue set in while continuing the financial assistance programme (Greece).

For those countries not under a financial assistance programme, or not undergoing severe macroeconomic adjustment, the reform implementation index remained very low, a result which also holds for the United States and Japan. This suggests that implementation of reforms suggested by international organisations is generally low and that the European Semester was not able to improve this situation.

By studying the OECD reform responsiveness rate, which is available for more countries and for a longer time-period than the European Semester implementation rate, the regression analysis by Terzi (2015) suggests that an International Monetary Fund programme, a high unemployment rate and financial market stress all tend to increase reform efforts.

Other indicators, such as the widely used 'ease of doing business' ranking of the World Bank, confirm that euro area countries, which faced severe macroeconomic adjustment problems and/or were under financial assistance programmes, have indeed implemented various reforms, which improved business conditions (Figure 7.5). Ireland had an excellent ranking before the crisis and therefore the reform need was much lower.

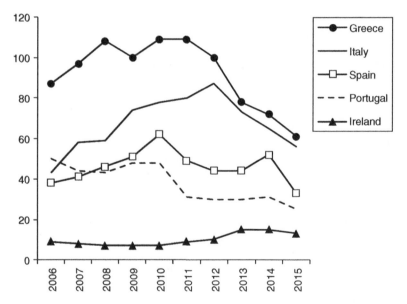

Note: 1 = most business-friendly regulations. Data from 153 countries in 2006, and 189 countries in 2015.

Source: World Bank.

Figure 7.5   World Bank 'ease of doing business' ranking, 2006–2015

7.1.3 Further Plans to Improve Structural Reform Implementation in the EU

The Five Presidents' Report (European Commission 2015) set out a plan for strengthening the Economic and Monetary Union. The report included two specific proposals with the aim of fostering structural reforms: the introduction of national competitiveness authorities, and formalizing and making more binding the convergence process.

My view is very positive about the establishment of national competitiveness authorities, an idea which was first proposed by Sapir and Wolff (2015). The competitiveness authorities would assess wage and productivity developments and economic reforms to foster competitiveness, while their European network should help to exchange views on best practices. I see the establishment of national competitiveness councils as a kind of decentralization, through which reform priorities would be defined nationally. It will likely increase the ownership of the reform process because a conclusion by such a national council could be seen by the national parliament and the government as a recommendation coming from inside the country, but not as an intrusion from Brussels. I do not think that the network of these authorities will be able to better internalize the cross-country implications of national structural policies, yet it will be a major improvement compared to the current governance framework even if the national authorities will primarily focus on the domestic consequences of the reform process.

On the other hand, my view is negative on the plan to formalize the convergence process and make it more binding. The idea of the Five Presidents' Report is to agree on 'a set of common high-level standards that would be defined in EU legislation, as sovereignty over policies of common concern would be shared and strong decision-making at euro area level would be established'. While setting benchmarks may be useful, structural reforms cannot be objectively measured. I also see difficulties in enforcement and making the system binding if a country does not meet the standards by the agreed time.

7.2 CONCLUSIONS

I draw three key conclusions. First, the European economic governance framework in fostering structural reforms failed before the crisis, and while the new framework has improved significantly with the introduction of the Macroeconomic Imbalance Procedure, so far it has been rather ineffective.

Second, pre-crisis euro periphery problems are well understood now, and Central and Eastern European countries therefore have a better chance to avoid such problems after joining the euro. In fact, Slovakia is thriving within the euro area, despite it joining the euro at perhaps the worst possible time: its conversion exchange rate to the euro was fixed in summer 2008 when CEE currencies were historically strong. Slovakian developments show that it is possible to thrive within the euro area when good structural policies are adopted.

Third, which is a corollary of the first conclusion, national economic policymakers should not expect too much from the European framework to steer their structural reform policies. The most promising new institution in my view is the planned establishment of national competitiveness authorities, which can improve the diagnosis of possible competitiveness problems and can help to identify the remedies. A network of these institutions can help to spread knowledge about best practices. I therefore advise CEE policymakers to establish truly independent and well-staffed national competiveness authorities and to encourage them to participate actively in their European network.

NOTES

*   Figures 7.2, 7.3 and 7.4 and some conclusions in this chapter were originally published in a paper provided at the request of the Committee on Economic and Monetary Affairs of the European Parliament and commissioned by the Directorate-General for Internal Policies of the Union and supervised by its Economic Governance Support Unit (EGOV). The opinions expressed in this chapter are the sole responsibility of the authors and do not necessarily represent the official position of the European Parliament. The original paper is available free of charge on the European Parliament's webpage, http://www.europarl.europa.eu/RegData/etudes/IDAN/2015/542677/IPOL_IDA(2015)542677_EN.pdf. © European Union, 2015.

1.   Key exceptions were the Czech Republic and Slovakia, and to a lesser extent, Poland.
2.   In late 2008, the ECB signed agreements with the central banks of Hungary and Poland on a euro repo facility, which did not involve a change in currency denomination (in contrast to the main request of the CEE central banks). The only benefit of the euro repo was that the CEE central banks could support their domestic banks with euro liquidity without giving the impression of falling foreign exchange reserves.
3.   German current account surpluses became excessive in the early 2000s, after having been in line with model predictions in the preceding three decades, according to the estimates of Darvas (2015).
4.   To be more precise, the exchange rate of the euro depreciated somewhat during the crisis, thereby boosting extra-euro exports of all euro area members. But arguably, the depreciation of the euro was much milder compared to what would have happened to, for example, the Greek drachma if Greece had had a stand-alone currency in 2008. Moreover, about half of the trade of euro area periphery countries is with rest of the euro area and therefore exchange rate adjustment cannot be used to correct the price and wage divergences with respect to, for example, Germany.
5.   See more details at http://ec.europa.eu/europe2020/making-it-happen/index_en.htm.
6.   See Regulation (EU) No 1175/2011 of the European Parliament and of the Council of

16 November 2011 amending Council Regulation (EC) No 1466/97 on the strengthening of the surveillance of budgetary positions and the surveillance and coordination of economic policies, which was part of the so-called 'Six Pack' adopted in 2011.

REFERENCES

Ahearne, A., J. Delgado and J. von Weizsäcker (2008), 'A Tail of Two Countries', Bruegel Policy Brief 2008/04.

Darvas, Z. (2009), 'The EU's Role in Supporting Crisis-Hit Countries in Central and Eastern Europe', Bruegel Policy Contribution 2009/17.

Darvas, Z. (2012), 'Intra-Euro Rebalancing is Inevitable, but Insufficient', Bruegel Policy Contribution 2012/15.

Darvas, Z. (2015), 'The Grand Divergence: Global and European Current Account Surpluses', Bruegel Working Paper 2015/8.

Darvas, Z. and A. Leandro (2015), 'Economic Policy Coordination in the Euro Area under the European Semester', briefing paper prepared for the European Parliament's Economic and Monetary Affairs Committee for the Economic Dialogue with the President of the Eurogroup, 10 November.

Darvas, Z. and G. Szapáry (2010), 'Euro Area Enlargement and Euro Adoption Strategies', in M. Buti, S. Deroose, V. Gaspar and J. Nogueira Martins (eds), *The Euro: The First Decade*, Cambridge: Cambridge University Press, pp. 823–69.

Darvas, Z. and E. Vihriälä (2013), 'Does the European Semester Deliver the Right Policy Advice?', Bruegel Policy Contribution 2013/12.

European Commission (2015), 'The Five Presidents' Report: Completing Europe's Economic and Monetary Union', Report by Jean-Claude Juncker in close cooperation with Donald Tusk, Jeroen Dijsselbloem, Mario Draghi and Martin Schulz, Brussels.

Sapir, A. and G.B. Wolff (2015), 'Euro-Area Governance: What to Reform and How to Do It', Bruegel Policy Brief 2015/01.

Terzi, A. (2015), 'Is the ECB sacrificing reforms on the altar of inflation?', Bruegel blog, http://bruegel.org/2015/03/is-the-ecb-sacrificing-reforms-on-the-altar-of-inflation/.

8. EU structural policies today: missing piece of the growth puzzle, or wishful thinking?

Brian Pinto*

8.1 WHAT IS STRUCTURAL POLICY?

There are two ways of looking at structural policy in the European Union (EU): the first is as the missing piece of the puzzle to get growth going; the second is to recognize, based on the emerging market experience, that structural policy typically entails upfront costs, which makes it hard to implement, especially in the presence of a debt overhang. In this case, the debt overhang may have to be resolved first. This is one of the main conclusions of this chapter. The second main conclusion is that the timing of structural policy matters. Structural policy is easier to implement in good times, and is much harder to implement once an economy is already in the midst of a crisis.

Economists who have spent most of their careers working on emerging markets are well acquainted with the term 'structural policies', or structural adjustment policy, to be more precise. In the emerging market context, structural policy grew out of the recognition that macroeconomic stabilization and 'getting the prices right', typically through import liberalization, may not be sufficient to put countries on faster growth trajectories. Other impediments to growth and private investment needed to be removed. The list included property and creditor rights, competition policy, a good legal and regulatory framework, flexible labour markets, and credible fiscal and financial institutions. The associated policy conditionality became an integral part of the World Bank's Structural Adjustment Loans, or SALs.

Given this background, discussing structural policies with a special focus on the European economy may be puzzling. After all, the euro area and EU countries are mostly advanced economies, or 'developed markets', and surely they already have the necessary institutions and structural policies in place. A related question is: why the emphasis on structural policy now, why not earlier when the euro area was being formed?

Obviously, the slow recovery of the EU and the euro area in particular from the global financial crisis of 2008–09 has much to do with the current focus on structural policy. As the president of the European Central Bank (ECB), Mario Draghi, underlined during a speech in May 2015:

> In every press conference since I became ECB President, I have ended the introductory statement with a call to accelerate structural reforms in Europe . . . The term 'structural reforms' is actually mentioned in approximately one third of all speeches by various members of the ECB Executive Board. By comparison, it features in only about 2 per cent of speeches by Governors of the Federal Reserve.

Perhaps not by coincidence, Draghi became ECB president in November 2011 when Greece was in meltdown, Italian sovereign ten-year bond spreads had crossed the so-called psychological threshold of 7 per cent, and there was genuine concern about the very survival of the euro.

In view of the amorphousness surrounding the term 'structural policy' in the developed market (as opposed to the emerging market) context, my strategy will be to allude to a few prominent recent papers on structural policy and then draw conclusions for the euro area as well as Central, Eastern and South-Eastern Europe (CESEE). By a process of elimination, I shall apply the term 'structural policy' to everything in economic policy that remains after excluding macroeconomic stabilization and 'getting the prices right'. In particular, what remains includes credible fiscal and financial institutions, policies for creating more dynamic and flexible economies, in both resource allocation and reallocation, managing volatility or the capacity to respond to economic shocks, and the microeconomic foundations of growth. I will stress the latter in this chapter.

8.2 FOUR PAPERS ON STRUCTURAL POLICY

The four papers I shall focus on are:

- A 2013 paper by Marek Belka on how joining the EU helped to transform Poland's economy.
- A 2015 speech by Mario Draghi making the case that structural reforms in the EU would have a big pay-off with the ECB's accommodative monetary policy stance and therefore should not be delayed.
- A 2014 paper by Christian Dustmann and co-authors on how wage restraint forced by the high cost of reunification and the competitive pressure from the transition to a market economy in Central

Europe, combined with a tradition of highly decentralized wage and work hour setting, was the pivotal factor in Germany's economic resurgence.
● The 2015 CESEE regional economic issues report of the International Monetary Fund (IMF).

8.2.1 Belka (2013)

The first paper, by Marek Belka (2013), is about how joining the EU transformed Poland's economy. The Polish case is important because it was the only economy to exhibit positive growth in the EU-27 during 2009, the nadir of the global financial crisis. Belka's main point is that neoclassical convergence, financial and trade integration, plus EU structural funds have combined to transform Poland's economy and achieve excellent economic results. Notable outcomes have been inward foreign direct investment (FDI) accompanied by innovation, manifested in vastly improved export quality and variety. Poland has become part of the European value chain and is fortunate in its geography with its close location to Germany. In fact, Germany accounts for more than 25 per cent of Polish foreign trade.

From this chapter's perspective, a prime question raised by Belka's analysis is the following: were any special 'industrial policy' interventions implemented to achieve Poland's good outcomes, apart from joining the EU? The answer is no. Poland in fact implemented the usual structural policies, achieving macroeconomic stabilization, ensuring property rights, fostering good fiscal and financial institutions and the like. In short, the standard list you would find in any World Bank- or IMF-supported programme.

But a close examination showed there was something much subtler. Neoclassical convergence obviously helped since Poland was poorer than its counterparts, Hungary and the Czech Republic, in Central Europe when the economic transition began there in 1990. But to attribute Poland's success primarily to neoclassical convergence would be too simplistic, as argued in Pinto (2014, Chapter 4). If convergence worked so well and automatically, one would expect all poor countries to grow rapidly and catch up with the rich countries, and we know this not to be the case. To the contrary, as set out in Pritchett (1997), we have had major divergence, accentuating income gaps between rich and poorer countries.

To fully understand what drove Poland's resilience during the global financial crisis as well as its much-envied record of unbroken positive growth since 1992, one has to turn the clock back 26 years to 1990. Poland's good economic outcomes were driven by a beneficial combination of:

- well-managed public finances;
- hard budgets for firms and banks, vigorous import competition and competitive real exchange rates; and
- sound management of volatility with the building up of fiscal space and foreign exchange reserves over time as the result of consistently good policies and 'staying the course'.

This policy combination plus good geography has worked extremely well for Poland. However, two not-so-obvious observations are worth making about the Polish growth experience.

First, the attitude under the 'big-bang' Balcerowicz programme (named for its architect, Leszek Balcerowicz) towards the large state-owned enterprises and banks was uncompromisingly Schumpeterian. In particular, the second item in the list above, which I call the 'micropolicy trio' (Pinto 2014), played a crucial role in fostering restructuring among large state-owned enterprises (SOEs), documented in Pinto et al. (1993). The process of hardening budgets in line with Kornai (1986) was multifaceted and dynamic, involving the following:

- unambiguous signals from the Ministry of Finance from day one that there would no bailout of any SOE no matter how big or politically connected;
- the imposition of a compulsory, fixed dividend on the portion of founding capital contributed by the government; and
- eventually, a change in the governance of banks to prevent new lending to loss-making SOEs.

At the same time, almost immediate import liberalization gave the SOEs little breathing room and forced efficiency by giving them a Darwinian choice between adapting to market forces or going bankrupt.

But the programme was also marked by pragmatism: the exchange rate of the zloty to the US dollar, which had been fixed in January 1990 as an anchor for price stabilization, was devalued 17 months later when it became apparent that the SOEs needed breathing room following the unexpectedly early collapse of Council for Mutual Economic Assistance (CMEA) trade (that is, foreign trade conducted under protocols observed by the Former Soviet Union and its satellite states, which guaranteed Polish SOEs easy foreign market access). And SOEs were allowed to sell off unused assets, which helped with resource reallocation by providing new, private start-up firms with machinery and equipment.

Nevertheless, hard budgets and import competition had huge short-run costs, with Polish gross domestic product (GDP) falling by a cumulative 18 per cent in 1990 and 1991 before growth resumed; with the much-maligned large SOEs in the forefront of the turnaround. This raises the question of whether the euro area has the appetite for large-scale Schumpeterian creative destruction as part of rejuvenating growth.

The second aspect of Poland's growth was that it was undoubtedly helped by the 50 per cent write-down of its official debts. It would have been hard to implement such drastic reform without the prospect of a large debt write-down that helped to clean the official books. In this context, access to EU Structural Funds was obviously a big plus as it enabled large public investments without requiring new debt to be issued. In other words, the implementation of hard budgets and product market competition was facilitated by the elimination of Poland's debt overhang. This offers food for thought in the euro area today (see below).

The core structural reform that Poland implemented, therefore, was to implement hard budget constraints for firms and banks, instantly increase product market competition, and adopt a pragmatic exchange rate policy. This was not easy to do because of the high short-run costs, but produced a big pay-off by forcing firms (even while remaining state-owned) and banks to innovate and move closer to the global technological frontier, thereby strengthening the microeconomic foundations of growth and raising potential growth.[1]

8.2.2   Draghi (2015)

The second paper is the text of Draghi's (2015) speech on structural reform referred to earlier. For Draghi, the purpose of structural reform is twofold: first, to raise potential growth by creating a climate for higher capital accumulation (increasing capital–labour ratios) and faster total factor productivity (TFP) growth; and second, to enhance resilience, thereby enabling quick rebounds and minimizing output losses following adverse shocks. The latter consideration is paramount, given the fear of hysteresis associated with the global financial crisis, highlighted in their study of the evolution of output after recessions in advanced economies by Blanchard et al. (2015).

Draghi further argues that there is no excuse for procrastination because the ECB's accommodative monetary policy, consisting of policy interest rates at the zero lower bound (ZLB) and quantitative easing (QE) (sovereign bond QE was started in March 2015), should facilitate structural reform by increasing the pay-off in terms of faster growth and investment benefits. In view of its importance and the need for consistent efforts across countries in a monetary union, he even proposes a centralized structure to govern structural reform: 'I believe there is a strong case for governance of structural reforms to be exercised jointly at the euro area level: to help each country to achieve the necessary level of resilience; and to ensure that they maintain that resilience permanently.'

It is relatively easy to critique Draghi on structural reform. First, he clearly defines the goals of structural reform, namely, to increase potential growth and resilience; but what is structural reform? He mentions only 'best practice across labour and product markets, tax policy and pensions'. Perhaps this will deliver faster growth and resilience; but one has to show how, and how quickly. And borrowing from Poland's experience, will this include uncompromisingly hard budgets to spur innovation and resource reallocation? This would help to increase TFP growth, but could also entail heavy short-run social costs.

Second, Draghi argues that accommodative monetary policy, by keeping long-term interest rates low and increasing liquidity, should facilitate structural reform by increasing the pay-off to structural reform through quick wins on investment and growth. But consider the opposite angle: that excessive leverage and a debt overhang in the euro area have compelled an accommodative monetary policy. Besides, supply-side factors, including adverse demographics, could have contributed to a steady decline in potential growth. To make the point, let us write potential growth g^* as the following function:

$$g^* = f(TFP, K, demographics)$$

where TFP is total factor productivity, K represents the capital stock and its accumulation and demographics feed into labour supply (and indirectly into the NAIRU, or non-accelerating inflation rate of unemployment) and potential output.

But the demand side could also exert its influence by affecting the path of K adversely. In particular, if government and private balance sheets are highly leveraged, then household demand may decline, firms may be unwilling to invest, and banks may be reluctant to lend (apart from being intertwined with the sovereign). This could lower g^* through the K channel, compounding supply-side effects, and also affect TFP growth adversely to the extent that new technology is embodied in new investment. In this case, the debt overhang has to be resolved first.

Indeed, Corsetti et al. (2015) argue in a VoxEU report that monetary policy has reached its limits in the euro area, and that growth is anaemic because of the debt overhang, which must therefore be eliminated. The authors propose several options, including securitizing a part of future tax revenues or even seigniorage to bring government debt-to-GDP levels below 95 per cent of GDP. The quid pro quo would be a reform in fiscal governance and the official bailout mechanism to make the tattered 'no-bailout clause' credible at last.

However, none of the debt restructuring proposals argues for a reduction in the net present value (NPV) of outstanding debt claims, without which it is hard to see how the debt overhang can be resolved. This demonstrates that, as with the hardening of budgets for firms and banks Polish-style, debt reduction is not a palatable alternative. This brings us back to square one, because with a debt overhang and low potential growth, the alternatives for ensuring sustainable debt dynamics are either debt restructuring or an indefinite adherence to accommodative monetary policy (policy rates at ZLB and QE).

Third, the idea that structural reform would increase resilience and allow quick recoveries from adverse shocks raises the topic of the timing of the reform. If it is to possess a countercyclical property, it needs to be implemented in good times, as with countercyclical fiscal policy. Fiscal cushions, sound banks, strong balance sheets – these are the foundations of resilience, enabling shocks to be absorbed and permitting quick rebounds after a recession; but these need to be in place before the adverse shock hits.

I would draw three conclusions from Draghi (2015). First, structural reform must be hard politically, because if there were quick returns to structural reform and doing it was easy at the ZLB and with QE (as Draghi argues) then we should have seen much more of it by now. Second, structural reform is going to be most effective when: (1) countries are far from the global technological frontier; (2) there is no debt overhang; and (3) such reform is implemented in good times. These assumptions do not hold in advanced euro area economies such as Italy. Third, for the same reasons, structural reform will be particularly effective in CESEE, because their leverage is lower and they remain far from the technological frontier.

8.2.3   Dustmann et al. (2014)

The third paper is by Dustmann, Fitzenberger, Schonberg and Spitz-Oener on Germany's transformation from 'sick man of Europe' to superstar. The authors' explanation revolves around exceptional flexibility and decentralization, right down to the firm level, in wage setting and work hours. Their story stresses three factors:

- The high reunification tab, which amounted to €900 billion over 1991–2003, approximately 50 per cent of average annual GDP, became a drag on economic performance and probably dampened expectations of wage increases.

- The transition to a market economy in, and the opening up of, four Central European economies (CE4: Poland, Czech Republic, Slovakia and Hungary) provided German firms with the option to source inputs from the CE4 or even relocate manufacturing there, keeping a lid on wage growth.
- 'German firms have always had the option not to recognize a union contract and to pay wages below the union wage, provided their employees accepted this.'

The eventual consequence was that unit labour costs fell in tradable manufacturing because of rising productivity, ability to source inputs from the CE4 and wage compression (especially of wages below median wage levels) in non-tradable and tradable services, which fed into the increase in manufacturing competitiveness. This propelled German growth.

Interestingly, the authors do not attach much importance to the 2003 Hartz Reforms or euro adoption in explaining German competitiveness. With regard to Hartz, they argue that these reforms came well after the process of wage decentralization and increase in competitiveness had begun in the 1990s, spurred by the reunification tab and the transition in the CE4. Moreover, the goal of the Hartz Reforms was to increase incentives for seeking employment, not to promote wage restraint, which was the decisive factor behind Germany's elevation to superstar economic status. In fact, the 'hard budget constraint' created by the unification costs and pressure from the CE4 probably facilitated the Hartz Reforms.

But the authors' argument about the adoption of the euro as a common currency not being an important factor is less persuasive. Without the euro, countries such as Italy, Greece, Spain and Portugal would have faced much higher borrowing costs before the global financial crisis, and more pressure to reform. Further, Germany would have needed to endure much greater wage restraint if countries such as Italy had been able to depreciate their currencies after the global financial crisis, which was not possible in the common currency regime.

Nevertheless, the main point of Dustmann et al. is hard to contest: that it is better to have wage flexibility than to lay off workers during a crisis or a difficult transition, because this helps to preserve human capital and skills during downturns, minimizing hysteresis. However, as the authors note, wage inequality could rise, as in Germany, and labour mobility may be impeded if workers need to stay at the same firm in order to be compensated when the good times return.

CESEE has a history of worker involvement in strategic decisions of firms and compensation structure. In Poland, wages were set at the enterprise level and were highly flexible during the early 1990s, restricted by the 'excess wage bill tax', better known by its Polish acronym PPWW,[2] once transition began. So the culture of work sharing and willingness to cut wages to preserve jobs is not alien. Interestingly, Draghi (2015) expresses a preference for wage and working-hour flexibility over dismissals during downturns.

8.2.4 IMF (2015)

This IMF report on CESEE equates a flexible labour market with easy hiring and firing practices. This protects investment during downturns, especially when firms are overleveraged. But in the euro area context, this position raises a difficult question: if there is a debt overhang and potential growth has been scaled back to 1 per cent (half the level before the global financial crisis), is it better to protect investment by firing workers (which will also reduce aggregate demand further) or to address the debt overhang directly? The obvious answer is that it is better to resolve the debt overhang directly. And along with this, one could go the German route described in Dustmann et al. of promoting flexible wages and work-sharing, an approach espoused by Draghi (2015).

The IMF (2015) recognizes excess leverage as an impediment that needs to be addressed in some CESEE countries. This makes complete sense. It is hard to implement structural reform without fiscal space in the presence of a debt overhang because there is no shock absorption capacity and structural reform tends to have upfront costs. This is where Draghi is too sanguine about the benefits of structural reform, even at the ZLB.

8.3 CONCLUSIONS

The main conclusion for the euro area is that the debt overhang may have to be resolved before one can think of benefits accruing from structural policy. The first reason is that structural reforms entail upfront costs and it is difficult to absorb these when a debt overhang is present. The second reason is that with potential growth having been reduced to just 1 per cent in the euro area, it is unlikely to grow out of its debt problem even with nominal policy rates at the ZLB, because the equilibrium real rate may be much lower than -2 per cent (2 per cent being the inflation target).

The second conclusion relates to the bifurcation between the United States (US) and the euro area, which became pronounced after the global financial crisis but was actually present much earlier, as attested by the 2003 Sapir Report on European growth. The Sapir Report (Aghion et al.

2003) concluded that euro area growth policy suffered in comparison with the US. Conclusion: good structural policies must be in place before a crisis hits. Indeed, even fiscal and financial institutions remain incomplete in the euro area.

My next set of conclusions pertains to CESEE. CESEE, especially the CE4, is well positioned to benefit from structural policy, being far from the global technological frontier with a limited or no debt overhang and generally good governance and institutions. It is better to implement structural policy from a position of strength. But what is structural policy? Mainly 2 to 5 in the list below, with 2 and 4 pertaining to the microeconomic foundations of growth:

1. Well-managed public finances to spur convergence in capital–labour ratios (raise public savings, invest in infrastructure, make good use of EU funds).
2. Hard budgets and import and domestic and regional competition to spur convergence in TFP by creating incentives to move closer to the global technological frontier.
3. Management of volatility to prevent crises or permit quick rebounds from them (good fiscal and financial institutions, fiscal and monetary space, higher national savings).
4. Flexible labour markets with emphasis on wages and working hours to protect investment and preserve worker skills during downturns, also enhancing resilience.
5. Resolving legacy issues (notably, excess leverage) to help keep up aggregate demand.

Lastly, I end with a question regarding CESEE, and a dilemma. The question is the following: how can structural policy across CESEE be coordinated to open up markets and FDI, and adopt 'best practice' policies? Is CESEE ready for greater regional competition?

The dilemma is this: if CESEE is the best it can be, could this make life easier or harder for the euro area periphery? My guess is that it will make the economic problems in the periphery much harder to solve because a bigger effort will be required to restore competitiveness and resolve the debt overhang.

NOTES

* This chapter is based on my presentation at the October 2015 joint conference of Narodowy Bank Polski and Oesterreichische Nationalbank on the Future of the

European Economy. I acknowledge helpful comments from Mariusz Sumlinski, but all interpretations and errors are exclusively my own.

1. Convergence based on distance from the global technological frontier is an idea developed by Philippe Aghion and his coauthors. Aghion and Durlauf (2009) discuss the growth policy implications.
2. PPWW = Podatek od ponadnormatywnych wypłat wynagrodzeń.

REFERENCES

Aghion, P., G. Bertola, M. Hellwig, J. Pisani-Ferry, A. Sapir, J. Vinals and H. Wallace (2003), *An Agenda for a Growing Europe: The Sapir Report*, Oxford: Oxford University Press.

Aghion, P. and S. Durlauf (2009), 'From Growth Theory to Policy Design', Commission on Growth and Development Working Paper no. 57, Washington, DC: World Bank.

Belka, M. (2013), 'How Poland's EU Membership Helped Transform its Economy', Group of Thirty Occasional Paper 88, Washington, DC.

Blanchard, O., E. Cerutti and L. Summers (2015), 'Inflation and Activity – Two Explorations and Their Monetary Policy Implications', IMF Working Paper, WP/15/230.

Corsetti, G., L. Feld, P. Lane, L. Reichlin, H. Rey, D. Vayanos and B. Weder di Mauro (2015), *A New Start for the Euro Area: Dealing with Debt*, VoxEU.org Book. http://www.voxeu.org/sites/default/files/Monitoring%20the%20euro area. pdf.

Draghi, M. (2015), 'Structural Reforms, Inflation and Monetary Policy', European Central Bank, Introductory speech at the ECB Forum on Central Banking in Sintra, Portugal, 22 May.

Dustmann, C., B. Fitzenberger, U. Schonberg and A. Spitz-Oener (2014), 'From Sick Man of Europe to Economic Superstar: Germany's Resurgent Economy', *Journal of Economic Perspectives* 28(1), 167–88.

IMF (2015), 'Central, Eastern and Southeastern Europe. Regional Economic Issues', May.

Kornai, J. (1986), 'The Soft Budget Constraint', *Kyklos* 39(1), 3–30.

Pinto, B. (2014), *How Does My Country Grow? Economic Advice Through Story-Telling*, Oxford: Oxford University Press.

Pinto, B., M. Belka and S. Krajewski (1993), 'Transforming State Enterprises in Poland: Evidence on Adjustment by Manufacturing Firms', *Brookings Papers on Economic Activity* 24(1), 213–70.

Pritchett, L. (1997), 'Divergence, Big Time', *Journal of Economic Perspectives* 11(3), 3–17.

9. EU structural policies and euro adoption in CEE countries

Anna Kosior and Michał Rubaszek

A country faced with a possibility of adopting the euro faces a decision problem: it must assess domestic strengths and weaknesses against the threats and challenges posed by the euro zone's structural and institutional features. This framing of the decision-making problem can be directly derived from the optimum currency area theory proposed by Mundell (1961), according to which entering the euro area creates an opportunity of accelerated growth through more trade and investment, and it also poses a threat of increased macroeconomic volatility arising from the loss of monetary independence. This theory argues that the success of euro adoption thus depends on two factors. First, on discrepancies between the country adopting the euro and the common currency area in terms of development level, economic structure and institutions governing the functioning of the economy. Second, on the existence and workings of mechanisms, both on a country and the euro area level, which could diminish risks related to limited domestic policy space following euro adoption. This multi-factor decision-making problem is further complicated by the fact that it has many moving parts, given that the structures of the euro area and the potential candidate economies are evolving over time, as are their institutional underpinnings.

Below we apply the above decision-making problem to the Central Eastern European countries (CEEC) that remain outside the euro zone, with the aim of identifying the role played by the European Union (EU) and national structural policies in the process of fostering convergence and preparing for euro adoption. Section 9.1 focuses on the implications of the euro area's current institutional design for the balance of risks related to euro adoption. In particular, we discuss to what extent this balance has changed with the progress made in terms of euro area institutional reforms since the financial crisis of 2008 and its aftermath. Section 9.2 investigates whether the fundamentals of the CEE economies are strong enough to participate in the 'competition between countries' fostered by the current institutional framework of the euro area. Section 9.3 discusses what kind of policies would make adopting the euro more attractive for the CEEC that are still outside the euro area. Section 9.4 concludes.

9.1   INSTITUTIONAL DESIGN OF EMU THROUGH THE LENS OF CATCHING-UP ECONOMIES

To frame the discussion, we differentiate between two types of currency union: a 'single-currency economic and monetary union' (EMU) (type 1) and a 'common-currency EMU' (type 2). Those two concepts should be understood as Max Weber's 'ideal types'.

The main characteristic of a type 1 currency union is that its monetary policy is accompanied by fully decentralized decision-making in other domains of economic policy. This arrangement is based on the principle that the prosperity of each country within the single currency bloc is solely a function of the quality and efficacy of domestic economic policies. There is an underlying assumption that the soundness of these policies will be a necessary outcome of national competition on a single market. As such, a type 1 currency union does not foresee risk- and burden-sharing between member states. In particular, it excludes any financial support, of either a temporary or a permanent nature, for member states facing difficulties.

The type 2 arrangement assumes that the prosperity of a member state is strongly influenced by the initial discrepancies in the quality of domestic institutions and production factors, that is, more generally by its history and geography. It also acknowledges that market-based incentives for sound economic policies at the national level can be too weak to produce good policy outcomes. As a result, this institutional model foresees substantial risk-sharing and mechanisms for creating a level playing field not only through temporary support during crisis but also as a means for compensating for heterogonous starting points. Such financial support is meant to prevent a permanent divergence of real incomes that could jeopardize the union's political integrity. The soundness of domestic economic policies in this model is seen as an outcome of greater control by the centre. Moreover, the type 2 arrangement recognizes the need for some centralized decision-making in policy areas that generate a large risk of externalities or spillovers under a single monetary policy (for example, in the area of financial supervision).

At its inception, the euro area closely resembled the single-currency economic and monetary union. Although the conspicuous structural and institutional heterogeneity of member states signalled the risk that a single monetary policy would have a destabilizing impact on individual economies, such fears were disregarded on several grounds. First, the risk of excessive indebtedness stemming from too-low interest rates was hoped to be effectively mitigated by the no-bailout clause and financial market discipline, on the one hand, and by the fiscal rules and national financial supervisors and regulators, on the other. Second, it was argued that increased competitive pressures related to euro area membership would foster structural reforms in the least-developed member states, thus strengthening their adjustment capacity to both asymmetric and common shocks. The reasoning was based on expectations of strong electoral pressure on governments that would find few other options to stabilize aggregate demand with no direct control of monetary policy and constraints put on fiscal policy (in line with 'there is no alternative' or 'reform or die'; see discussion in Bean 1998). It was also assumed that increased price transparency would lower product or labour market rents to be captured by insiders, thus decreasing resistance to reform (Blanchard and Giavazzi 2003). Third, the capacity to smoothly adjust to shocks was also expected to benefit from improvements in fundamentals of the less-developed currency union members resulting from higher capital inflows. Fourth, increased trade flows between euro area member states were supposed to lead to lasting convergence of their business cycles (Frankel and Rose 1998). All in all, fast transformation of the euro area economies into a highly integrated region, characterized by relatively low convergence gaps, was to guarantee that the single monetary policy of the European Central Bank (ECB) would fit them all and help them to remain on a balanced growth path. Moreover, the expectations that the euro area would be a macroeconomically and financially stable region with no risk of systemic crises justified the absence of crisis management, resolution and financing mechanisms at the euro area level.

The financial crisis of 2009 painfully verified the validity of those assumptions. Decentralized financial supervision had turned out to be ineffective in preventing credit and asset price booms in some member states. Given credit risk mispricing by financial markets, fiscal rules did not prevent procyclical policies. Moreover, although in some cases reforms that could permanently lift productivity and remove structural rigidities were indeed facilitated by euro adoption (Alesina et al. 2010), they were not widespread. As a result, since the introduction of the euro several economies had been closing gaps in gross domestic product (GDP) per capita at the cost of gradual deterioration of competitiveness, debt accumulation and growing risks to their banking sector's stability. When the financial crisis hit, those countries experienced deep recessions and banking crises that turned into sovereign debt crises. Since such developments were inconsistent with the assumptions underlying a single-currency EMU and the institutional design of the euro area, the tools that could effectively reduce the resulting contagion and fears of the euro area break-up were initially limited.

The response of the EU to the crisis was based on a series of reforms, which put the euro area on the path towards a common-currency EMU. The analysis of the progress from type 1 to type 2 currency union indicates that the key changes to the euro area's institutional set-up included: (1) creation of the banking union; (2) expansion of the ECB's tools; (3) establishing crisis financing mechanisms; and (4) strengthened centralized surveillance of domestic economic policies.

First, creation of the banking union. The decision to introduce a single currency without at the same time centralizing banking sector oversight was motivated politically and running counter to the early drafts of the institutional underpinnings of the euro area (James 2012). Moving the locus of decision-making about the banking sector to the euro area level is a big step towards establishing federal structures in the currency union. Compared to the situation when supervision was organized fully along national lines, the current set-up should reduce supervisory forbearance (including leniency towards 'national champions') and result in less tolerance to overgrown banking sectors and excessive risk-taking by banks. In addition, the banking union will work towards greater risk- and burden-sharing among currency union members and a more homogenous monetary policy transmission mechanism.

Second, expansion of the ECB's tools. The lack of political unanimity regarding the ECB's mandate initially limited the central banks' crisis fighting armoury to interest rate cuts and liquidity provisions to the banking sector (reflected in the widening of TARGET2 positions), which proved insufficient in preventing the self-fulfilling liquidity crises in the sovereign debt markets. With the start of sovereign debt bond purchases by the ECB, the scale of risk-sharing between euro area member states has increased substantially.

Third, establishing crisis financing mechanisms. The permanent crisis financing mechanism in the form of the European Stability Mechanism is compatible with the notion that macroeconomic and financial stability will not always be assured in a heterogonous currency union, despite strengthened governance; hence there may be a need for temporary financial support for member states facing financial difficulties.

Fourth, strengthened centralized surveillance of domestic economic policies. Reforms of the euro area governance framework were multifaceted: national fiscal policy frameworks were strengthened, and the European fiscal rules became more nuanced. In particular, more focus was put on reducing public debt and changing the structural fiscal balance rather than the nominal fiscal deficit of the public sector. The scope and tools for the central oversight of domestic policies were expanded. Under the reformed Stability and Growth Pact, the power of the European Commission (EC) to apply sanctions for breaking fiscal rules has increased, and under the Macroeconomic Imbalance Procedure the EC was empowered to extend its surveillance over the broader set of economic policies, to issue recommendations for corrective actions and to propose fines for non-compliance. Moreover, with the introduction of the 'Two-Pack' legislation, the Commission was given the authority to review and require amendments to draft budgetary plans of member states as well as to issue proposals on the need to initiate a financial assistance and macroeconomic adjustment programme in a given country. All in all, the euro area moved towards a greater importance of centralized surveillance over domestic policies as a tool of promoting the soundness of these policies.

It should be noted that the institutional changes in the above-mentioned areas have not been finalized. An important element of the banking union, the European Deposit Insurance Scheme, is still at the planning stage and it is not clear whether there will be enough political support for implementing it. There is also a conviction that the fiscal governance framework (that is, the number rules of the Stability and Growth Pact and the way they are implemented in practice) have become very complex and opaque. Moreover, the oversight of domestic policies affecting member states' macroeconomic stability (competitiveness) is very weak. As a result, further reforms in those areas are envisaged (Juncker 2015). Moreover, several crucial features of the type 2 EMU are missing. First, rigid solidarity mechanisms to prevent divergence in structurally weaker member states are absent. Second, most economic policies remain at the national level, and financial markets and competition on a single market are implicitly ascribed the main disciplining role over those policies. This suggests that the balance of risks related to euro adoption may be tilted to the downside for less-developed economies, characterized by weaker institutions.

9.2 ARE CEEC READY FOR COMPETITION WITHIN THE EURO ZONE?

The experience of several euro area countries suggests that fulfilling the Maastricht criteria does not guarantee success within the euro area. Other factors are crucial for keeping an economy on a balanced growth path. We argue that the following characteristics should be taken into consideration (a more detailed discussion is outlined in Kosior and Rubaszek 2014): structural competitiveness and the convergence process; and similarity of institutions and structures. In this section we discuss why these factors are important for a country planning to join type 1 EMU, which was described in the previous section.

9.2.1 Structural Competitiveness and the Convergence Process

It might be argued that successful membership in type 1 EMU depends predominantly on the strength of a country's cost and structural competitiveness. The former can be measured by relative wages, whereas for the latter there is no universally accepted definition. It usually refers to the quality and diversity of a country's export potential, which in turn depends on the business environment, human and social capital, and the innovativeness of the economy. The economic literature provides evidence that structural competitiveness is crucial over the longer horizon, whereas cost competitiveness is more relevant for short-run analyses. For example, Kaldor (1978) shows that countries gaining export market shares tend to experience appreciation rather than depreciation of the real exchange rate. Moreover, as indicated by Montobbio and Rampa (2005), cost competitiveness is more important for low-tech sectors, whereas structural competitiveness is more important for high-tech sectors.

Currently, labour costs in CEEC stand at very attractive levels: hourly wages are more than three times lower than in the euro area (Table 9.1). This cost advantage is reflected in a relatively high share of low-tech sectors in the structure of CEEC exports, which makes it more sensitive to changes in relative costs compared to other euro area economies. This prompts the question: how well are CEEC prepared for wage convergence after euro adoption? This question is relevant as the economic motivation of euro area accession is essentially acceleration of the convergence process, including narrowing of the wage gap. We can infer from the experience of selected euro area countries that the loss of cost competitiveness might aggravate macroeconomic imbalances if it is not counterbalanced by increases in structural competitiveness. Moreover, the adjustment process is more painful within EMU than under a floating exchange rate regime, where external competitiveness can be easily regained through exchange rate depreciation. In a currency union, internal price and wage adjustments are necessary to restore external equilibrium, and their impact on aggregate demand is likely to be more detrimental in a country with a structurally uncompetitive production structure. For this reason, a big challenge for CEEC is to enhance their structural competitiveness, which is currently relatively low: the Innovation Union Scoreboard for 2015 shows that CEEC are doing much worse than developed euro area countries (Figure 9.1).

Table 9.1   Hourly labour costs (business economy, €, 2014)

EA	PL	CZ	HU	RO	BG	HR
29.2	8.2	9.6	7.8	4.8	3.8	9.3

Note: BG = Bulgaria. CZ = Czech Republic. EA = euro area. HR = Croatia.
HU = Hungary. PL = Poland. RO = Romania.

Source: Eurostat.

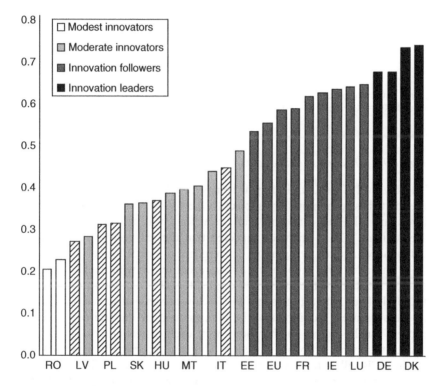

Note: DE = Germany. DK = Denmark. EE = Estonia. EU = European Union. FR =
France. HU = Hungary. IE = Ireland. IT = Italy. LU = Luxembourg. MT = Malta. PL =
Poland. RO = Romania. SK = Slovakia.

Source: European Commission.

Figure 9.1   EU Innovation Scoreboard 2015

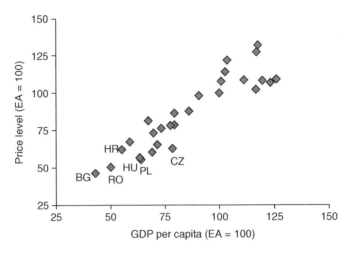

Note: BG = Bulgaria. CZ = Czech Republic. HR = Croatia. HU = Hungary. PL = Poland. RO = Romania.

Source: Eurostat.

Figure 9.2   *Real and nominal convergence in EU countries in 2014*

The low level of structural competitiveness of CEEC is intertwined with the fact that these economies are subject to the convergence process. As price levels and GDP per capita are well below the levels prevailing in the euro area (Figure 9.2), it might be expected that the real convergence process will be accompanied by a gradual convergence of prices, hence higher inflation. This additional inflationary pressure, combined with the fact that the interest rates set by the ECB are the same for all EMU countries, will put the level of real interest rates in CEEC below the level observed on average in the euro area. Additionally, the management of the real convergence process usually requires higher, not lower, levels of real interest rates. As a result, it is highly probable that after adopting the euro, interest rates set by the ECB will be too low in relation to the needs of the CEE economies.

If interest rates set by the ECB are too low for the needs of CEEC, this will pose the risk of building up macroeconomic imbalances, among others, in the form of a real estate bubble. Angello and Schuknecht (2009) show that the level of short-term interest rates is one of the major factors explaining the likelihood of the real estate bubble. It can be argued that the low level of the real interest rate was the main factor behind the creation of the real estate bubble in Spain and Ireland. Moreover, in the case of CEEC the risk of a real estate bubble is enhanced by the underdevelopment of the private rental market. To conclude, low structural competitiveness and the convergence process are factors that are increasing the risk that after euro adoption CEEC will experience a gradual build-up of macroeconomic imbalances.

9.2.2 Similarity of Institutions and Structures

The experience of selected countries shows that structural and institutional diversity might be an important source of business cycle divergence in relation to other members of the monetary union, leading to a situation in which the single monetary policy is not adequate for the cyclical situation of the economy. The reasons are twofold. First, differences in economic institutions and structures may be a source of asymmetric shocks. Second, the heterogeneity of the institutions and structures might lead to a different response of member states to common shocks. This will pose a difficulty for the ECB as the lack of differences in the functioning of the monetary policy transmission mechanism is a crucial condition for effective monetary policy in a currency union (Guiso et al. 1999). Consequently, in the absence of deeper integration in the euro area, institutional and structural differences of CEEC in comparison to major euro area economies may constitute a challenge for the smooth functioning of their economies after single currency adoption.

The literature on the monetary transmission mechanism points to a series of factors that influence the response of the economy to macroeconomic shocks. In this section we will focus on only one factor, just to illustrate the problem. In particular we will discuss the consequences of private rental market underdevelopment. As evidenced in Figure 9.3, the CEEC are characterized by a very low share of households that acquire housing services through the private rental market. While in 2014 tenants represented more than one-fifth of all households in the euro area, the share of tenants stood below 5 per cent in all CEEC but the Czech Republic.

In countries characterized by a high share of owned apartments, financial market liberalization or interest rate decline will probably have a more pronounced impact on credit dynamics, housing demand and economic activity than in countries characterized by a high share of rented apartments. For example, Cuerpo et al. (2014) show that a well-developed private rental market limits the response of housing prices to interest rate changes. Simulating a dynamic stochastic general equilibrium (DSGE) model, Rubio (2014) in turn finds that countries with a low share of the rental market experience higher volatility of GDP and inflation and a different response to a monetary policy shock than countries with a higher share of tenants. The existence of an effective rental market may also have important implications for financial stability. After all, low-income households are relatively

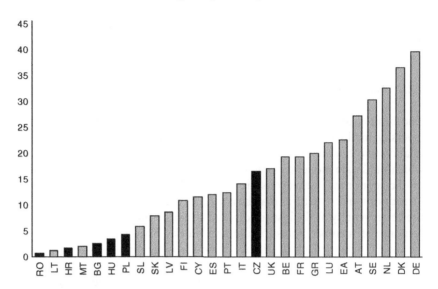

Note: AT = Austria. BE = Belgium. BG = Bulgaria. CY = Cyprus. CZ = Czech Republic. DE = Germany. DK = Denmark. EA = euro area. ES = Spain. FI = Finland. FR = France. GR = Greece. HR = Croatia. HU = Hungary. IT = Italy. LT = Lithuania. LU = Luxembourg. LV = Latvia. MT = Malta. NL =Netherlands. PL = Poland. RO = Romania. SE = Sweden. SK = Slovakia. SI = Slovenia. UK = United Kingdom.

Source: Eurostat.

Figure 9.3   The share of households living in rented (at market price) apartments in 2014

more sensitive to adverse income changes over the business cycle. As a result, the possibility to acquire housing services by this group of consumers through renting rather than buying with a mortgage limits the scale of adjustment of the housing market during the economic downturn. To summarize, one can expect that differences between euro area countries in terms of private rental market development (and other institutions related to the functioning of product and labour markets) will be reflected in the asymmetry of monetary policy transmission and cyclical divergence.

9.3   WHAT CAN BE DONE TO MAKE THE EURO AREA ATTRACTIVE FOR CEEC?

Given the economic challenges of euro adoption discussed in the previous section it should not be surprising that public support in CEEC for

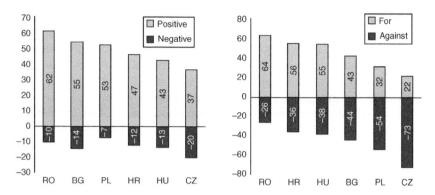

Note: BG = Bulgaria. CZ = Czech Republic. HR = Croatia. HU = Hungary. PL =
Poland. RO = Romania.

Source: Eurobarometer, July 2015.

Figure 9.4   Attitude towards the EU (left panel) and support for the euro (right panel)

the euro is much lower than for the EU, especially in Poland and the
Czech Republic (Figure 9.4). The question then arises: what can be done
to make the euro area attractive for CEEC? We claim that there are two
options. The first is to make EMU more integrated, that is, to progress
towards the type 2 EMU. The second option, which is discussed in this
section, is to strengthen structural competitiveness and adjust the structure of CEEC economies to the reality of functioning inside the euro
area.

   The first challenge of euro adoption by CEEC relates to a gradual
build-up of macroeconomic imbalances. The risk of macroeconomic
imbalances might, however, be reduced by enhancing structural competitiveness. So far, the modernization of CEEC economies has been mainly
driven by the adoption of foreign technologies, which were imbedded both
in foreign direct investment and in imports of capital goods by domestic
companies. This kind of innovation policy was reflected by the low share
of research and development (R&D) expenditures in GDP in CEEC in
comparison to the euro area average. As indicated by Montobbio and
Rampa (2005), for developing countries, creating new products through
internal R&D is not crucial for technological upgrading. However, for a
country that aims at competing with the group of developed economies
that are close to the technological frontier, such as euro area member states,
this kind of innovation policy might lead to low international competitiveness, unless substantial wage gaps persist. The challenge for CEEC prior

to euro adoption is thus to enhance the business environment towards promoting risky, innovation activities. This can be done through national policies aimed at improving labour and product market regulations, as well as investing in human and social capital (Andrews and Criscuolo 2013). Enhancing the innovativeness of CEEC could also be supported by improving the management of innovation process, for example through creating a Competitiveness Authority, as proposed in the Five Presidents' Report (Juncker 2015). This kind of institution would be responsible for coordinating and evaluating innovation policy at the country level. Apart from the national efforts, EU-wide policy could also be a factor contributing to an improvement in the competitiveness structure in CEEC. In particular, the Multiannual Financial Framework for the years 2014–2020 contains more funding aimed at promoting internal R&D and cooperation of firms with research institutions than in the EU budget for the years 2007–2013. These funds, if deliberately used, might be an important source of financing the transformation of the CEEC competitiveness model from a 'low-cost' into a 'quality-based' one.

The second challenge relates to the risk of cyclical divergence. This risk depends on the degree of similarity of economic institutions and structures. In type 1 EMU, economic policy is conducted at the country level and is subject to a soft coordination process among the EU member states within the European Semester. Most regulations influencing the functioning of labour or product markets are not harmonized. Moreover, the guidelines from European institutions, in particular recommendations under the European Semester, are not very informative about how to adjust institutions to limit the risk of cyclical divergence of CEEC after euro adoption. Adjusting the European governance framework towards better support for CEEC preparation to adopt the euro could proceed by reformulation of recommendations and guidelines, so that they better reflect the importance of a given change in policy for the functioning of the EU or the euro area as an entire region. The EC's proposal to revamp the European Semester by better integrating the euro area and national dimensions is a welcome step in this direction. At the country level, policymakers could explicitly take into account whether the implemented economic policies are making the country more or less adjusted to functioning within the euro area. Given the example from the previous section, policies in CEEC that are promoting home ownership rather than the development of the rental market will make the potential decision on the euro adoption more difficult in the future.

9.4 CONCLUSIONS

In this chapter we have argued that the probability of CEEC success after euro adoption depends on two factors: the institutional design of the euro area, and the fundamentals of CEEC economies. In the case of the former the key question is whether the paradigm of EMU is built around competition or the solidarity principle. In the competitive, type 1 model, it is essential that accession to the euro area is preceded by measures to strengthen the structural competitiveness of CEEC and adjust the structure of their economies to the conditions necessary for functioning efficiently within the currency union. Otherwise, as the experience of the recent crisis has shown, the single currency could increase the risk of macroeconomic imbalances and cyclical divergence, which could slow down the economic development of the country temporarily or even permanently.

REFERENCES

Alesina, A., S. Ardagna and V. Galasso (2010), 'The Euro and Structural Reforms', in A. Alesina and F. Giavazzi (eds), *Europe and the Euro*, Chicago, IL: University of Chicago Press and Cambridge, MA: National Bureau of Economic Research, pp. 57–93.

Andrews, D. and C. Criscuolo (2013), 'Knowledge-Based Capital, Innovation and Resource Allocation: A Going for Growth Report', OECD Economic Policy Papers 4.

Angello, L. and L. Schuknecht (2009), 'Booms and Busts in Housing Markets. Determinants and Implications', ECB Working Paper Series 1071.

Bean, C. (1998), 'The Interaction of Aggregate-Demand Policies and Labour Market Reform', *Swedish Economic Policy Review* 5(2), 353–82.

Blanchard, O. and F. Giavazzi (2003), 'Macroeconomic Effects of Regulation and Deregulation in Goods and Labor Markets', *Quarterly Journal of Economics* 118(3), 879–907.

Cuerpo, C., P. Pontuch and S. Kalantaryan (2014), 'Rental Market Regulation in the European Union', European Economy – Economic Papers 515, European Commission.

Frankel, J.A. and A.K. Rose (1998), 'The Endogeneity of the Optimum Currency Area Criteria', *Economic Journal* 108(449), 1009–25.

Guiso, L., A. Kashyap, F. Panetta and D. Terlizze (1999), 'Will a Common European Monetary Policy have Asymmetric Effects?', *Economic Perspectives* Q4, 56–75.

James, H. (2012), *Making the European Monetary Union*, Cambridge, MA: Harvard University Press.

Juncker, J.-C. (2015), 'Preparing for Next Steps on Better Economic Governance in the Euro Area', in close cooperation with Donald Tusk, Jeroen Dijsselbloom, Mario Draghi and Martin Schultz. http://ec.europa.eu/priorities/economic-monetary-union/docs/5-presidents-report_en.pdf.

Kaldor, N. (1978), 'The Effect of Devaluation on Trade in Manufactures', in N. Kaldor, *Further Essays in Applied Economics*, London: Duckworth, pp. 99–116.

Kosior, A. and M. Rubaszek (eds) (2014), 'The Economic Challenges of Poland's Integration with the Euro Area', National Bank of Poland. https://www.nbp.pl/en/publikacje/inne/The-economic-challenges-of-Poland-s-integration-with-the-euro-area.pdf.

Montobbio, F. and F. Rampa (2005), 'The Impact of Technology and Structural Change on Export Performance in Nine Developing Countries', *World Development* 33(4), 527–47.

Mundell, R. (1961), 'A Theory of Optimum Currency Areas', *American Economic Review* 51(4), 657–65.

Rubio, M. (2014), 'Housing-Market Heterogeneity in a Monetary Union', *Journal of International Money and Finance* 40(C), 163–84.

PART IV

Labour market and productivity
developments

10. Labour market integration and associated issues: Kipling is wrong

Peter Sinclair

'East is east and west is west, and ne'er the twain shall meet.' So wrote Rudyard Kipling in 1889. As far as Europe is concerned, Kipling's dictum was tragically true until 1989–91. Now, we rejoice in the fact that it is true no longer, at least as far as commerce and travel are concerned. It is also becoming steadily less true of labour markets, a principal subject of this chapter, as well.

There are 22 Central, Eastern and South-Eastern European (CESEE) countries. What they share is two things: geographical contiguity, and a generally unlamented legacy of several decades under communism. Their economies are all described as 'emerging'. But they are very heterogeneous. Gross domestic product (GDP) per head at market exchange rates in one of them is nearly ten times higher than in another. Inflation and unemployment rates are almost as diverse, as are their institutional features. All but eight of them represent fragments of two states that vanished late last century: the Soviet Union and Yugoslavia. Two emerged after the break-up of Czechoslovakia. Half of the 22 have joined the European Union in this century. In some cases this has meant nuancing their new-found independence by swapping one form of supranational or federal politico-economic structure for another. Five participate in the euro zone. Two more use the euro informally, and another two are very tightly linked to it by euro-based currency boards.

This chapter will focus very largely on the 11 CESEE countries that have joined the European Union (EU), and also upon their EU partners. How have the economic experiences of the 11 varied between each other, and in comparison with how other EU members have fared? What differences distinguish the recent economic performance of euro zone members, whether CESEE or not, from their other EU partners? What lessons can be learnt, and what implications for future policy follow?

10.1 THE CURATE'S EGG: EXCELLENT IN PARTS

The twenty-first century macroeconomic record of the EU countries, east and west, is patchy. An 1895 Punch cartoon, squarely in the tradition of the Barsetshire Chronicles of Anthony Trollope (1855–67), depicts a young person having breakfast with the bishop and his wife. The parson, a curate, is struggling with an egg. The bishop is concerned and asks if there is something wrong with it. 'No, my lord: parts of it are excellent!' the curate replies. The EU macroeconomy is unfortunately therefore something of a Curate's Egg.

One excellent part of the egg relates to the evolution of real wage rates and living standards in the cohort of East European countries that joined the EU on 1 May 2004. Poland is the largest of these countries. Data compiled by the Organisation for Economic Co-operation and Development (OECD) reveal that Poland's average real wage rate per employee (measured in US dollars, at constant 2012 prices and at purchasing power parity exchange rates) increased from under half (about 47 per cent) of Germany's in 2000 to over 54 per cent in 2014. The Czech and Slovak Republic comparisons with France depict faster convergence between these dates, with their ratios of French wages rising by a quarter. In Hungary, where macroeconomic performance at the time of the global financial crisis in 2008 was highly disturbed, there is evidence of still faster catch-up in wages in this period, against the euro zone's third-largest economy, Italy: here, the wage gap almost halved. The Slovenia–Italy comparison (for 2003–14) is similar.

The size-weighted average of wages in these six CESEE economies appears to have risen by almost 25 per cent so far this century, relative to the size-weighted average of the big four EU economies of France, Germany, Italy and the United Kingdom (hereinafter referred to as FGIU; from 45 per cent to 56 per cent). So this measure of the wage gap displays a half-life of about 40 to 45 years, assuming exponential decay persisting at this rate. Furthermore, the fact that these real wage comparisons are at purchasing power parity (PPP) rather than market exchange rates definitely understates the speed of convergence, at least from the standpoint of tradable goods producers' perceptions of the price of labour.

In fact, it is not true that the OECD dataset paints a picture of national-average real wage differentials narrowing across the board. In the smallest two economies of the pre-2004 EU, Ireland and Luxembourg, wages were well above the FGIU average in 2000, and have actually risen far faster since then. If countries with lower wage rates do display some broad tendency to catch up, wage rates have also been growing noticeably faster in small economies than in bigger ones. Smaller polities may be nimbler in reacting to shocks; they may win tax competition contests because bigger neighbours fail to notice or respond to their actions; or their gains in this period may be ephemeral and due simply to luck.

These observations enable us to say that the CESEE economies that joined the EU in 2004 have exhibited unmistakable progress to labour market integration on this measure. Very similar results are found for rates of real GDP growth. How much of this evidence of progress, on wages or growth, might have occurred without EU accession, however, is very hard to guess at this stage, and detailed econometric studies of both issues have yet to appear. But studies of what EU accession seems to have done for economic growth rates of latecomers that entered the EU in the 1970s and 1980s find a small but significantly positive boost in most cases.[1] This is what the phased removal of trade barriers should generally lead us to expect. If corroboration be sought, the growth rate differential in the past decade between FGIU on the one side, and the CESEE countries that joined in 2004, appears to be somewhat larger than might be expected on the basis of the central tendencies of convergence reported on the basis of worldwide regressions by, for example, Doppelhofer et al. (2004).

Indicators of labour market integration are not just restricted to wage rates, however. Quantities matter, too. It is instructive to see what has happened to levels of employment among CESEE members of the EU, and for other EU countries. What do the data tell us?

Suppose we consider what happened to employment as a whole in the 28 countries that now make up the EU in the six years following the global financial crisis in 2008. We can split these 28 countries various ways. One is to focus on the 19 that now comprise the euro zone, and contrast them with the nine that remain outside it. In the nine outsiders, Eurostat data show that employment increased by 108 000 between 2008 and 2014. But among the 28, taken as a whole, it fell by 4 997 000. It is here that we encounter a far from excellent part of the Curate's Egg.

Euro zone countries saw very heavy net job destruction, on a scale not really seen since the aftermath of the Second World War, or in peacetime, the 1930s. But non-members as a whole created them. Let us inspect some aspects of these stark differences country by country. Between 2008 and 2010, employment rose in only three of the larger countries, Austria, Belgium, and Germany, and in each case only slightly, by 1 per cent or less; it also increased in three small economies, Cyprus, Luxembourg and Malta. Everywhere else, it fell in this two-year period.

When countries face an unexpected downwards jolt in the demand for labour, as so many did as a result of the global financial crisis in 2008, some combination of employment and real wage rates has to respond. Real wage rates can hold up, as a result of the pattern of contracts, legal

restrictions, trade union intervention, or rigidities and generosity of benefits. But the price for that is inevitably a sharp fall, possibly delayed a little
by anti-firing laws, in the number of jobs. Alternatively, it may be pay that
takes the strain, with employment holding up. And there is a continuum of
possibilities in between. No one can claim that one type of reaction is necessarily superior to another. This said, this author deems it better, if only
on the basis of fairness across families, generations and income groups, to
let pay bear the larger adjustment downwards. One consequence of that
response is that measures of labour productivity could record sharp – if
temporary – declines.[2]

In the four years from 2010 the pattern could hardly have been more
different from the period 2008–10. Only nine of the 28 EU countries witnessed an absolute decline in employment. Four of these nine – Bulgaria,
Italy, Romania and the Netherlands – saw only modest declines of just
over 2 per cent or less. The other five were, like Italy, all direct victims to
varying extents of the European debt crisis; and Bulgaria and Romania,
in common with other CESEE countries outside the EU such as Albania,
Macedonia and Serbia, suffered major collateral damage from the catastro-
phe that befell Greece. One of those five was, like Bulgaria and Romania, a
CESEE country: Slovenia. The others were Cyprus, Greece, Portugal and
Spain. These five saw their employment levels shrink by at least 8 per cent;
in Greece's case, nearly one in five jobs were lost in these years. The largest
absolute fall, of 1.4 million, occurred in Spain.

By contrast, employment jumped by over 1 million in both Germany
and the United Kingdom (UK) from 2010 to 2014. The fastest propor-
tionate rises in these years occurred in Malta (almost 12 per cent) and
Luxembourg and Sweden (over 5 per cent); the three Baltic states saw
employment bounce back vigorously by 3 or 4 per cent, after previous sharp declines. Some of the contrasting labour market fortunes of
the EU-28 are due to intra-union migration. In the UK's robust labour
market, for example, a majority of the new jobs were secured by nationals
from EU partner countries, predominantly from the CESEE area; German
and Luxembourg data paint a similar picture. Much as one might regret
the role of 'push' factors that often helped to engender it, this too must
count as an instance of successful integration. Against this, unemployment, to which I now turn, remains a stubborn problem in much of the
EU, especially but not only in the Southern countries outside the CESEE
group.

The north–south divide in the pre-2004 EU is to some degree mirrored
in the group of its new CESEE members. Here the levels and dynamics of
real wages, productivity, GDP per head and employment, north of a line
from the Pyrenees to the Danube, broadly speaking, all tend to display

considerably greater strength than south of it. Moldova, the poorest CESEE country by most definitions, and north of the Danube estuary, is an exception. So, it seems, is Belarus. But economic growth rates within the CESEE area on both sides of the Danube have been quite rapid, despite variations over time and space.

Along with its generally disappointing unemployment performance, the EU's overall record of economic growth from 2008 to 2015 has had the character of a prolonged and deepening recession. In the EU-28, OECD data imply that real GDP per head at constant market prices shrank by almost 1.3 per cent from 2008 to 2014 – a fifth of 1 per cent per annum – in contrast to gains close to 3 per cent in Canada, Japan, Mexico and the United States. Within the EU, the picture varies. The CESEE members of the OECD generally fared much better than the old western core. The Czech Republic, Estonia, Hungary, the Slovak Republic and Poland all registered gains on this measure, with Poland topping the list by far, at over 16 per cent. In the west, Germany grew at 4 per cent, and Ireland, Sweden and the UK by about 1.5 per cent, but all the others, even Austria and Luxembourg, registered declines. In Greece, the cumulative slide in real income per head was almost one-fifth. Turning to the volumes of aggregate real GDP, as reported by Eurostat, Bulgaria and Romania have now recovered most of the early ground lost over this period. Only Croatia displays a time profile of persistent negative growth, though with a much milder decline than in Greece.

10.2 UNEMPLOYMENT – AND INFLATION

International migration, and internal demographic dynamics, imply that employment and unemployment, whether in absolute numbers or in rates, do not always have to move in opposite directions. But usually they do, and recent EU experience is no exception. Consider, first, the 15 countries that comprised the EU until the 2004 expansion. Five saw unemployment drop from 2010 to 2014, all of them from the prosperous north: Denmark, Germany, Ireland, Sweden and the UK. The other ten saw their unemployment rates increase. In Greece, by far the worst case, unemployment more than doubled from 12.7 per cent to 26.5 per cent on Eurostat data; in absolute numbers of extra souls out of work, Spain and Italy topped the table. Among the weakest countries, Greece, Portugal and Spain, unemployment rates had consistently exceeded the EU-15 average for decades. Their labour markets had never functioned well, and events in and after 2010 were to tip them still deeper into failure.

Among the 11 CESEE countries that joined the European Union in or after 2004, unemployment fell almost everywhere. The three exceptions lay in the Balkans: Bulgaria, Croatia and Slovenia, all of them caught in the backwash of the euro debt crisis. In the three big inflation targeters, the Czech Republic, Hungary and Poland, it ended down in the 6–9 per cent range. This is well below the 11.6 per cent average in the 12 initial euro zone members (despite the fact that their largest economy, Germany, saw unemployment tumble to 5 per cent). The biggest drops in unemployment rates from 2010 to 2014 occurred in the three Baltic States,[3] but to levels still above those prevailing in 2008.

In the late twentieth century, and in the early years of this century, unemployment rates in EU countries tended to move quite closely. From about 2007, things changed. If one contrasts the unweighted variance of national unemployment rates for the euro zone (12 countries) after 2007, with the seven years before that, a startling figure emerges: the statistic jumps tenfold. Why might that be? Broadly speaking, unemployment falls in Germany and some of its neighbours, where it was already quite low, and increases sharply in the troubled south, especially Greece and Spain. Part of the explanation must be that the euro debt crisis arose in some countries, but not others. The monetary system was unified but fiscal arrangements remained diverse, or became increasingly so. The crisis itself went on to drag down the exchange rate, which served to create more jobs in Germany's traded sectors. Yet the depreciated euro could do little to offset, first, the cumulative effects of previous declines in international competitiveness in the south, and later, the collapse of jobs in the area's finance, real estate and public sectors which had blossomed there (perilously, it was to transpire) in the euro's early years.

How have unemployment and inflation rates been related in the EU? Unemployment, like inflation, is endogenous, so the influence on the latter from the former is just one stage on a complex route, which is traced back to monetary or fiscal policy and, further, to the politico-social forces that underlie it. Nonetheless, understanding the unemployment–inflation link is of crucial importance. A fascinating recent paper by Gali (2015) compares Phillips curve relationships in the EU and the United States (US). The time dimension of his canvas is broad: it stretches back into the 1970s. Data are confronted by a sophisticated dynamic stochastic general equilibrium (DSGE) model. He asks how the EU and the US differ in the way inflation is linked to unemployment, and how this has changed over time. One of the phenomena he identifies is a general reduction in inflation rates associated with any level of unemployment. This has occurred in both sides of the North Atlantic. Another is hysteresis, which is apparent in the EU's unemployment rates, but not in the US. Past history matters in Europe, in a way it does not appear to in America. The EU Phillips curve, he finds, has flattened in recent years. Inflation is far less sensitive to unemployment than it used to be.

The spatial dimension in Gali's intriguing portrait, on the other hand, is narrow. The EU's data are geographically aggregated, and do not adjust for twenty-first-century accessions. This prompts questions about the inflation–unemployment relationships between different EU countries. Have they all flattened? How similar are they? Preliminary analysis of the individual country data confirms that all the EU-15 countries have seen their inflation rates fall for any given level of unemployment. This vertical shift down is strongest where inflation was highest in the late twentieth century, away from the Austria–Belgium–Denmark–Germany–Netherlands core, and above all in Iberia and Greece.

Yet while Germany's post-2000 Phillips curve does indeed seem flat, and France's nearly so, this is certainly not true of other EU countries. In Greece, Ireland, Italy, Portugal and Spain, simple bilateral regression lines (with inflation lagged by a year) display their pronounced traditionally negative slopes. And more than that, most of them also exhibit convexity. So the marginal effect on inflation of additional unemployment in these countries clearly appears to be diminishing, though much more slowly in some than in others. National Phillips curves have become more similar, both within the euro zone and outside it, but by and large they remain distinct.

Phillips curve diversity has interesting implications. It might testify to cross-country differences in inflation expectations, trade union density and power, wage negotiation systems, unemployment benefit rules, tax structures on earnings, patterns of structural change across sectors, and legal restrictions on hiring and firing. Unfortunately this author is not yet able to report any research results, whether of my own or by others, that could enable one to apportion relative importance to these variables. But the lingering diversity does also indicate that EU labour markets continue to retain distinguishing national features. Ironically, labour market integration with union partner countries is perhaps most advanced in the UK and Sweden, which remain outside the euro zone.

Convexity points to the principle that greater dispersion in national unemployment rates, all else equal, may tend to increase overall average inflation. When inflation is targeted, even tacitly, that suggests that monetary policy may become a little more aggressive than it would otherwise be, for a given path of aggregate unemployment or output gaps. With Taylor's principle counselling an above-unity long-run coefficient on inflation, and a much more modest one on unemployment, this could start to make a non-trivial difference to policy rates. Yet if the national Phillips curve is flat for a tightening large labour market such as Germany's, and downward-sloping for high-unemployment countries, as in the mid-2010s, one might see a bias towards expansionary rather than disinflationary setting of monetary policy instruments. In either case, the key point is that a monetary union's policy-makers may need to look carefully at the geographical breakdown of data and forecasts, and not just keep their eyes glued to the aggregates. The injunction to look at country-by-country details applies even more forcefully, as we shall see, to the financial stability and macroprudential adjuncts to monetary policy-making.

Inflation has been low and fairly steady in the twenty-first century thus far. Compared with the 1970s and 1980s, at least, this represents an achievement. But inflation rates have differed between EU countries, although much less than in the closing decades of the previous century. The euro zone was a monetary union, but not a union as far as inflation rates are concerned. Inflation has been more disturbed in the troubled south, especially in Greece. There it swung from well above average to sharply negative after 2010, in obedience to the country's evolving unemployment.

Greece's negative inflation has meant that the euro has turned out not to be a union of real exchange rates: between 2010 and April 2015, for example, Greece experienced real labour cost depreciation of 21 per cent according to International Monetary Fund (IMF) data. Italy, Portugal and Spain have also witnessed substantial falls. The problem here is transitional, but rather alarming. The slide in nominal wage rates and prices has been protracted; and hence, to a large degree, presumably anticipated. For a given nominal policy interest rate, this means substantially enlarged expected short-term real interest rates.

This phenomenon is known as the 'Walters critique'. With its nominal policy interest rate necessarily a single number for all its members, a monetary union may come to display destabilization, at least for a while.[4] Real interest rates must be lower (and thus providing a boost to spending) in areas with below-average unemployment. The opposite will occur in areas where unemployment is higher, where aggregate spending will be curbed by higher real interest rates. While the euro zone may have succeeded in its objective of squashing overall inflation rates (although that might very well have happened anyway), the architects of its monetary union had gambled on the absence of asymmetric disturbances to its constituent economies, which the Walters critique mechanism could otherwise only aggravate. From 2010 onwards, sad to say, they began to lose their wager. The much-heralded 'EU business cycle', that observers had so much hoped would be mild and uniform, simply disappeared. Boom areas such as Germany and its close neighbours saw unemployment tumble. But the EU's southern periphery underwent the steepest prolonged decline in GDP and employment for at least eight decades.

In fact that bold wager seems in retrospect to have been risky even in the euro's first few years. Back then, from 2000 to about 2008, it had been Germany's turn to be in the doldrums, along with the two other large economies, France and Italy, while the periphery, including Greece and Spain, ran merrily ahead. The wager might be rationalized on the hope that gains – from more intra-union trade and transparent competition and the greater liquidity and narrower spreads induced by financial market integration – could promote long-run growth. It is just conceivable (though very doubtful) that the euro zone's aggregated GDP might have grown even more slowly than it did after 2000, without such stimuli as monetary union might possibly have provided.

What had poisoned the chalice for Iberia, Italy and Greece from 2010? It is not just that the monetary union rules had banished the options to counter recession from 2010 by independent monetary expansion or nominal exchange rate depreciation. The unforeseen slide in world real interest rates implied that the scope for policy rate cuts in bad times for the European Central Bank (ECB) (and other central banks) was unexpectedly reduced: this was because of the zero bound, the convention that (nominal) policy rates could not be negative.[5]

On top of this, any opportunity for fiscal expansion in the troubled region was closed by the unfortunate 'torture mechanism' in the EU's Growth and Stability Pact rules (which required additional deflationary measures when a recession lowered tax receipts, once the ratios of debt or deficits to GDP had been breached). Furthermore, even without these rules, the risk premium on already high public sector debt might well have spiked up enough in free private capital markets to choke off any additional national government borrowing. Behind these countries' deepening recession from 2010 lay a real estate bubble in the previous decade. This must have been aggravated by two things: first, myopia and miscalculation about true real interest rates on the part of property buyers faced with far lower nominal interest charges on euro-denominated loans than they had been used to in the inflation-prone legacy currencies; and second, the imprudent eagerness of foreign banks to keep granting low-interest loans to the countries' already heavily indebted residents and governments.

10.3   THE EURO

With the benefit of hindsight, many policy-makers and observers in all euro zone countries, and beyond, are now starting to look back on the euro experiment as misconceived. But some of the hoped-for net benefits might conceivably appear in the future. History's verdict might well, eventually, be less negative. And for now, it seems to this author that there are powerful arguments in favour of maintaining the euro zone bloc intact. Let us consider some of them from the viewpoint of Greece.

First, the additional short-term employment that might be secured by the reintroduction of the Greek drachma would be bought by a large surge in inflation. Bringing inflation back down again after that would presumably entail a major loss of jobs, if only because promises of reduced inflation would lack credibility. Disinflation tends to cost more job-years than re-inflation engenders.

A second difficulty is that Greek official and private sector debts are denominated in euros. Exchange rate depreciation would certainly increase the nominal home-currency cost of servicing them. Adding in a plausible heightened risk premium would imply a higher discounted value of real servicing costs as well. Greece would remain in an 'original sin-bin'. There would be no scope for the gentleman's default of allowing creeping inflation to erode the ratio of its debts to its income.

A third challenge would stem from the observation, evident from most economic models, that a freely floating exchange rate, were Greece to adopt it perforce or by choice, is typically a dampener of shocks emanating from abroad, but an amplifier of shocks of domestic origin. And a fourth point is that Greek public opinion has remained favourable to the euro. The country's residents clearly appreciate the much greater stability to the path of their nominal price level since 2000, than in the previous decades when monetary policy decisions were taken at home.

Ironically, the single currency is more popular in its troubled southern member countries than elsewhere. This is perfectly consistent with the powerful analysis by Lucas (2000) of the consumption-equivalent losses agents appear to suffer from inflation. In Germany and other northern euro zone countries, average inflation rates after 2000 are not much below what they were before 2000. So for these countries' citizens, the euro has brought no appreciable fall in inflation. All it has done, it appears to them, is to raise the prospect of higher taxes to fund bailouts for the governments of other countries that had failed – repeatedly perhaps – to balance their books.

Then there are more general arguments for preserving the euro area. One is the value of waiting. Dissolution or fragmentation is irreversible. There is uncertainty. The weather could change. With luck, eschewing fragmentation today might mean avoiding it completely. Another relates to the extreme difficulty of holding the rest of the euro zone together, if Greece were to go. Financial market participants would immediately ask, 'Who's next?' Contagion was painfully obvious under the Exchange Rate Mechanism in 1992–93, let alone between Greece and other troubled members of the euro zone in and after 2011. So the single currency's guardians resemble the multi-store retailer which may be prepared, for reputation reasons, in a many-stage game, to go to enormous lengths to protect any of its outlets that is challenged. This celebrated industrial organization idea is known as the 'chain store paradox'.[6] And a third, rather different, point is that sunk costs are bygones, and should be regarded as such. The euro experiment would presumably never have been entered into, at least as far as the Mediterranean members are concerned, had the subsequent difficulties been foreseen. But the costs incurred in the past are over. That makes them irrelevant. The unfortunate experiment cannot now be undone. If policy is time-consistent, it is surely only the future that should matter now; however much that might set up a fascinating conflict between today's optimal plan for today and tomorrow, and tomorrow's optimal decision *ex post*.

For any non-member country considering whether to enter the exchange rate mechanism (which may both entitle and require it, later on, to adopt the euro), none of the above arguments apply. Agreeing that the existing euro zone needs to be preserved does not imply that it should expand. From the standpoint of a potential new member, entry is (all but) irreversible, so the value of preserving options – the value of waiting – will typically commend staying out for now. In time, we shall learn more: more about how the European debt crisis will have been resolved; more about whether members in fiscal emergencies can be assisted, rather than punished; more about whether financial stability threats will have been defanged by new institutions; more about further imponderables, such as whether the ECB will have proved able to surmount its challenges without the need for costly recapitalization.[7] But the 'value of waiting' argument may not apply to small countries, too miniscule to qualify as optimum currency areas on their own. They might have decided in the meantime, however – like the Baltic states or Montenegro – to find some route to euro-ization, one way or another.

Many observers of the euro project, both supporters and critics, unite to maintain that a monetary union will not work unless accompanied by some form of fiscal union. The supporters argue in favour of a fiscal union; the critics argue against both monetary union and fiscal union. What both groups may be imagining is a mechanism of intra-federal redistribution, which responds to weaker tax revenues in a region suffering a negative shock to income, with a partly compensating transfer from more fortunate regions. Such systems operate in Australia, Canada and the United States, and inside EU nation states as well. Concepts of fairness and economic efficiency point strongly towards a case for supporting a region or member country in acute difficulty, rather than insisting on its attempting to balance its books on a year-by-year basis, a policy which would only increase its burdens at just the worst time.

Nonetheless, there is a powerful case for countries within a monetary union to maintain a quite distinct armoury of fiscal instruments. This would be impossible if all such instruments had to be harmonized, and set in unison by a supranational fiscal authority. Farhi et al. (2011) show that a currency union country, unable to alter its exchange rate unilaterally, can still alter its fiscal instruments to replicate the effect of a devaluation. In their set-up, which resembles the micro-founded traded/non-traded model of an open economy explored by Neary (1980), you can increase value added tax (taken to be rebated on exports but applied on imports), and use the proceeds to subsidize employment. This way, external competitiveness can be restored, when damaged by relative inflation, with no damage to domestic employment. They describe their policy combination as 'fiscal devaluation'.[8]

Possible variants on this theme of fiscal devaluation are legion. They could include different rates of value added tax increase on different sets of products, cuts in national insurance levied on wage income that were skewed in favour of employees or employers, or subsidies limited to additional employment or the hiring of unemployed individuals, for example. In imperfect competition, changes in opposite directions on specific and *ad valorem* taxes can increase potential welfare. Under bilateral monopoly in labour markets with unions, a mix of specific subsidies and *ad valorem* taxes may make the union perceive a more elastic labour demand curve, leading to an increase in people at work.[9]

Implementing such ideas in the EU might call for some reinterpretation of the ban on 'state aid', as well as a reversal of the pressure that the European Commission has long exerted towards narrowing differences in countries' indirect tax regimes. There would also be questions to resolve. For example: whether fiscal devaluation measures could only be deployed as a last resort, and perhaps with general agreement, in conditions that the International Monetary Fund used to term 'fundamental disequilibrium'; or whether small changes in the vector of commodity and labour taxes could be made by any member country whenever it wished.

The central point is therefore this: permanent fixity of nominal exchange rates (at 1 to 1) is a *sine qua non* of monetary union, and a binding constraint; yet that need not preclude the use of two or more budgetary instruments which can resemble the now banned exchange rate changes. For these reasons, one must conclude that the view that a successful monetary union requires a full fiscal union can be dismissed as dangerously mistaken.

10.4 THE LESSONS FROM DETROIT

Urban magnets that once attracted, can start to repel. The city of Detroit in the US filed for bankruptcy in 2013. Thirty-eight years earlier, New York City came extraordinarily close to that humiliation. One factor at work in both cases is the mobility of taxpayers, whether individual or corporate. Detroit and New York were magnets in the mid-twentieth century. Detroit attracted large numbers of workers for its car factories in the 1940s and 1950s. New York City drew in migrants from a host of sources in Europe, from Puerto Rico, from upstate and from the farmlands and towns of many other parts of the union. For a while, the tax base grew fast enough to finance these cities' increasingly ambitious expenditures and welfare assistance projects. But in time, better-off residents came to notice that adjacent districts, outside the city's boundaries, levied lighter taxation. Many employers took advantage of interstate highways, and lower taxes, rents and congestion, to move out too. Suddenly a virtuous circle turned vicious.

In ensuing decades, Detroit's population would fall by more than 60 per cent. The city's debts would spiral on a per capita basis as residents fled, leaving debt servicing burdens to fall on a diminishing number of (generally poorer) families. Demographic changes in New York were more muted, while the flight of many higher-income families to prosperous Connecticut and New Jersey suburbs undermined not just the city's tax base, but the state's as well.

Until recently, leading Western European economies would respond to periodic surges in labour demand by attracting streams of immigrants from outside Europe. Starting in earnest in the 1960s, France would draw from its former colonies in North Africa; Germany primarily from Turkey; the United Kingdom from South Asia and the Caribbean. In the twentieth century, labour flows within the EU were modest. The UK, Sweden and Ireland opened their doors to job-seekers from the EU's new members in 2004, and substantial intra-EU migration began for the first time.

After the eruption of the European debt crisis, however, youth unemployment jumped sharply in Italy and Portugal, and far more, to over 50 per cent, in both Greece and Spain. While some of these countries' jobless young managed to move to other continents, chiefly North America, large numbers have been moving north to the countries with less moribund labour markets: France, Denmark, Sweden and, above all, Germany and the UK. These youthful migrants are often well-educated graduates, and (perhaps 'or') adventurous souls with pronounced entrepreneurial instincts. Like the better-off refugees from Detroit and New York City, many will therefore go on to earn large incomes, and contribute generously to income tax receipts in their host countries. The onus of servicing the debts of the governments of their source country will only rise for the diminishing numbers of residents that remain there.

The inference to be drawn from this is that some way should be found to break the vicious circle of substantial emigration by high-earning future taxpayers aggravating the debt burden of those who stay behind. One way of doing this might be as follows. A citizen of EU member country x who migrates to earn income in EU member country y could have income tax levied by (or shared with) y's fiscal authority, but at rates set by the government of country x, with transfers to that government (if needs be, under careful supervision to prevent diversion of the proceeds). Presumably legal obstacles would block any retrospective application of the proposed procedure, but at least future migrants' taxes could be channelled to their home country. And it would lessen the pressure on y's fiscal authorities to raise tax rates. Such rules could be applied only to a country suffering large net emigration, or to one facing serious fiscal challenges. Or they could be applied much more generally. It is worth noting in this context that in important new research, Alesina et al. (2015) find, perhaps surprisingly, that from 2009 to 2013, austerity-related tax increases have proved more damaging to domestic output than government expenditure cuts. These observations simply reinforce the conclusion that some forms of fiscal union could be full of unsuspected pitfalls.

10.5   CREATIVE ACCOUNTING, SUPERVISING BANKS, AND LIMITING OR FREEING CAPITAL MOVEMENTS

One common thread between the global financial crisis that erupted so violently in September 2008, and the European debt crisis that has rumbled on, menacingly, since then, is the awful temptation to hide embarrassments from balance sheets. First in the United States, and then elsewhere, accounting rule changes and the proliferation of opaque financial derivatives combined to allow commercial banks to park risk and risky activity, as they saw it, somewhere well away from the public gaze.

Governments got into a similar game. Accounts of what governments truly owed could be manipulated easily. Around the turn of the century, many of the pioneering dozen members of the fledgling euro zone found ingenious ways of presenting their balance sheets that would satisfy the Maastricht condition that government debt should not exceed 60 per cent of a year's GDP. Non-euro zone participants succumbed to similar seductions too. In the UK, the Public–Private Partnership, set up in 1998, concealed the London Underground railway investment spending from government accounts. The sorry saga that followed is well described in Chapter 14 of King and Crewe (2014).

Another British fiasco has been the Private Finance Initiative (PFI). This too is an ugly child of the 1990s. PFI deals have funded many hospital, school and prison construction projects. What has been purchased are two things: an illusion of low government spending; and timely, within-budget project completion. But the price has been grossly bloated quarter-century streams of rental payments and other fees paid to intermediaries which reflect a pattern of capital costs far above rates at which government can borrow. In April 2015, the *Independent*, a British newspaper, quantified these hidden debts at £222 billion. This immense sum exceeds the European Commission budgets for 2015 and 2016 combined, at the exchange rates prevailing at the date of writing. Financial creativity, and the woes it can beget later on, are no isolated Hellenic phenomenon.

In the banking arena, local regulators can be captured by the institutions in their purview. Tolerance and forbearance of dubious lending and other practices can ensue. In the US case, Agarwal et al. (2014) demonstrate how helpful involvement by national, federal supervisors can be in preventing them. Recent changes enacted through the new European System of Financial Supervision are replacing national by supranational inspection. This is greatly to be welcomed. So is the principle that the new rules should hold for all EU member countries, and not just the euro zone. Together with sharply increased minimum capital ratios, EU-wide coordinated and centralized supervision should serve to limit the risks of a systemic banking crisis originating inside the EU.

Retail banking systems vary between different EU countries. But national oligopolies are often the norm. Under some conditions – though not all – interest rate spreads should narrow when the number of sellers increases. If that happens, allowing a bank in country x to attract deposits and lend in country y should generate additional surplus for y's depositors and borrowers. When countries x and y are similar, cross-hauling can develop, with y's banks challenging incumbents in x, and possibly gains all round. When retail banks vary in costs and efficiency, the weakest may be forced to close. This opens the door for the chance of still further gains.

Yet history warns us to be careful. The narrowing of retail banking spreads is characteristic of the run-up to a banking crisis. Lower loan rates have an automatic tendency to reduce delinquency, which causes the more foolish bank boards to congratulate themselves on their apparently more successful methods of screening loan applicants, and therefore to lend still more aggressively, whenever allowed. Easier credit for mortgages fuels a real estate boom. And then: a crash. This pattern of events is so well documented in practice that one begins to wonder whether banking is perhaps an exception to the rule that vigorous competition should always be welfare-increasing.

In times of severe crisis affecting a specific euro zone country, the European authorities have imposed capital controls. This happened first in Cyprus in 2013, and then again in Greece in 2015. The Cypriot controls lasted almost two years in all; the Greek ones were more stringent, but more short-lived. The aim was to stem deposit withdrawals from any major retail bank operating there, and stop it from collapsing into insolvency. The infringement of the principle of unfettered capital mobility within the EU was regretted, but rightly deemed essential. Such controls operate in two ways. There are limits on the funds that can be transferred abroad, and restrictions on cash withdrawals from bank deposits. Bank runs are absolute anathema. One cannot challenge the case for stopping them in the Cypriot and Greek cases. The only question-mark relates to why, in the face of a protracted haemorrhage of deposits, action was not taken earlier.

But there is a big difference between suspending a depositor's right to liquidate claims (an absolute necessity but only in the severest of banking crises), and limiting their entitlement to transfer funds abroad (for which a somewhat more general case might be made). There will be a few central bankers still at work in France, Italy, Portugal and Spain, for example, and even in the UK, let alone Greece, with personal knowledge of how their countries' international capital controls operated. Systems differed, and evolved over time. Sometimes citizens could transact freely, in unlimited amounts, at a financial exchange rate designed to balance demand and supply continuously, and which differed, occasionally widely, from a commercial exchange rate for export and import payments. The old Belgium–Luxembourg dual exchange rate system is the classic model of this. In other examples, some or all categories of outward capital movements were simply banned. Outside the EU, Brazil and Chile have resorted to temporary taxes on outward or inward flows of capital, at modest rates, while many Asian countries, such as Indonesia, Malaysia and Thailand, have imposed quantitative restrictions or outright prohibitions for varying periods in this century after instances of crisis. A large majority of non-OECD countries, China and India included, still retain limits on at least some types of international capital movements.

In recent years the official attitude of the IMF has morphed noticeably from strict blanket opposition to such arrangements, into one of qualified acquiescence when circumstances made them seem necessary. A key question confronting EU policy-makers is whether their adherence to the notion of untrammelled intra-EU capital movements should also admit occasional exceptions; and perhaps not just at moments of extreme strain, such as for Greece in 2015.

There are several reasons for thinking that they should. One is the problem of differentially asymmetric information. A Ruritanian bank may be unable to observe all the characteristics of a Ruritanian loan applicant, but it is likely to have a distinctly better idea of whether to trust them than a bank from another European country. An outside newcomer bank is likelier to buy lemons. The outside bank from abroad may be keen to enter, and prepared to stomach initial losses from inevitable errors; stimulated perhaps by calculation that outcomes on these new loans are poorly correlated with those on other assets, or hopes of future gains from learning. The arrival of outside lenders will force local banks to shave their spreads and margins.

If things go really sour, local and newcomer banks may stay locked in a Stackelberg price war, playing a chicken game and desperately hoping that someone will have to drop out and let survivors' prices and profits recover. On top of that, if any were to fail, the lower bound on what it would itself have to provide against its liabilities will surely encourage greater risk-taking: 'heads I win, tails the taxpayer loses'. The arrival of a foreign bank may therefore make domestic incumbent banks act less prudently. This prompts the thought that retail banks headquartered in one EU country should not necessarily always be allowed to compete on equal terms in every other EU country. There could well be a cogent case for applying greater Basel-II style risk-weights (and hence enlarged minimum capital ratios) if it lends large amounts to residents of a less developed country with signs of macroeconomic stress, for example. And there is an even stronger case for 'gold-plating' such weightings within the EU. Facts must be faced. Loans from some EU countries to some other EU countries, whether to private or official borrowers, are not equally riskless. Nor do relative risks stay put. They can and do evolve. Uniform and constant riskiness throughout the European continent is a noble objective. It is certainly not yet a reality. Pretending otherwise is worse than folly. It is unpardonable.

Then there are the telling lessons provided by the model of Aoki et al. (2009). These authors look at the possible effects of removing capital controls on two types of country: first, those where the financial system is reasonably sophisticated; and second, those where it is not. A startling feature of their ingenious theoretical model is the very different macroeconomic evolution that these two types of economy may display. In the first, exposure to foreign lenders causes output to fall on impact, but later to register strong gains. In the second, a short-lived cheap-lending frenzy and a brief real estate boom push real income up for a while, but this happy time is followed by a very painful and prolonged recession. Twenty-first-century dynamics in Spain and Greece look like a copybook instance of the latter. But it bears emphasis that the Bank of Spain's courageous and (at the time) deeply unpopular insistence on its country's provisioning against foreseeable future loan losses by its banks (though sadly not the exempted *cajas* run by some foolish politicians) during its country's boom will have protected it from a far worse aftermath later on.

10.6   CONCLUSIONS

One conclusion to draw from the previous section is that though free movement of labour within the EU should be accepted as sacrosanct, the case for unfettered capital movement may be more open to doubt, at least at times of exceptional strain. Another is to welcome the new system of EU-wide supervision of banks, while keeping the door ajar for mildly handicapping a bank that lends heavily to residents of another EU country with warning signs (excessive credit growth or hints of a real estate bubble). Previous sections expounded arguments for rejecting a complete fiscal union, and instead espousing the possible benefits of fiscal devaluation for a country whose external competitiveness had been gravely impaired. There is a good case for shielding the euro zone from possible departures while advising possible future entrants to pause and wait for better news. Sections 10.1 and 10.2 chronicled and examined the tragedy of mass unemployment throughout much of the EU's southern countries, while celebrating the largely successful integration of the CESEE members' labour markets.

So Kipling was wrong. In the European continent today, at least, he would have a far better case for pessimism about the integration of Europe's north and south, than its east and west.

NOTES

1. For example, Martinez-Zarzoso and Sinclair (2001).
2. The UK was a country where pay dropped much more than employment, and remained weak for several years after 2010. The hourly labour productivity statistics told a sorry tale. Flexibility in real wage rates was accompanied by a sharp jump in the perceived marginal cost of capital, at least for smaller firms. So substitution of labour for capital, and for more as opposed to less labour-intensive products, appears to have played a major role. Many CESEE countries demonstrated not dissimilar phenomena at this time. But just how far did hourly labour productivity actually decline? The Office of National Statistics has revised its first estimates of quarterly changes upwards by a net total of 8 per cent across the period 2009–13 thus far.

3. These three countries suffered from a very steep but short-lived downturn, quickly reversed. The most extreme case, Latvia, is discussed in an illuminating paper by Blanchard et al. (2013).
4. If prices keep falling in the high-unemployment areas, compared to those where labour markets are overheated, spending patterns in both regions, and abroad, should eventually adjust to favour the products of the former.
5. In 2014, the ECB followed the lead of Sweden's Riksbank, in setting a slightly negative nominal interest rate on commercial banks' deposits lodged with it. The Riksbank pioneered this invasion of the zero bound in July 2009.
6. Analysed in Selten (1978).
7. As the introductory chapter (Ch.1, pp. 1–32) in Milton and Sinclair (2011) shows, central banks have in the past been able to roll along for several years with negative capital. Furthermore, the marked-to-market value of holdings of troubled member governments' bonds may of course recover from their modest current levels.
8. See also Farhi and Werning (2012).
9. As expounded, for example, by Sinclair (1987, Ch. 16).

REFERENCES

Agarwal, S., D. Lucca, A. Seru and F. Trebbi (2014), 'Inconsistent Regulators: Evidence from Banking', *Quarterly Journal of Economics* 129(2), 889–938.

Alesina, A., O. Barbiero, C. Favero, F. Giavazzi and M. Paradisi (2015), 'Austerity in 2009–2013', National Bureau of Economic Research Working Paper 20827.

Aoki, K., G. Benigno and N. Kiyotaki (2009), 'Capital Flows and Asset Prices', Centre for Economic Performance Discussion Paper 921.

Blanchard, O., M. Griffiths and B. Gruss (2013), 'Boom, Bust, Recovery: Forensics of the Latvia Crisis', *Brookings Papers on Economic Activity* 47(2), 325–88.

Doppelhofer, G., R. Miller and X. Sala-i-Martin (2004), 'Determinants of Long Run Growth: a Bayesian Averaging of Classical Estimates (BACE) Approach', *American Economic Review* 94(4), 813–35.

Farhi, E., G. Gopinath and O. Itskhoki (2011), 'Fiscal Devaluations', National Bureau of Economic Research Working Paper 17662.

Farhi, E. and I. Werning (2012), 'Fiscal Unions', National Bureau of Economic Research Working Paper 18280.

Gali, J. (2015), 'Hysteresis and the European Unemployment Problem Revisited', National Bureau of Economic Research Working Paper 21430.

King, A. and I. Crewe (2014), *The Blunders of Our Governments*, revised and updated edition, London: One World.

Kipling, R. (1889), 'The Ballad of East and West', first published as 'Kamal' by 'Yussuf' in *The Pioneer*, 2 December 1889; later in *The Sussex Edition of the Complete Works in Prose and Verse of Rudyard Kipling*, 35 vols, published 1937–39, London: Macmillan & Co., Vol. 32, p. 231.

Lucas, R. (2000), 'Inflation and Welfare', *Econometrica* 68(2), 247–74.

Martinez-Zarzoso, I. and P. Sinclair (2001), 'Transfers, Trade, Food and Growth: Britain and the European Union over 40 Years', in R. Broad and V. Preston (eds), *Moored to the Continent? Britain and European Integration*, London: University of London Institute for Historical Research, pp. 1–28.

Milton, S. and P. Sinclair (eds) (2011), *The Capital Needs of Central Banks*, London, UK and New York, USA: Routledge, Taylor & Francis Group.

Neary, J.P. (1980), 'Non-traded Goods and the Balance of Trade in a Temporary Keynesian Equilibrium', *Quarterly Journal of Economics* 95(3), 403–29.
Selten, R. (1978), 'The Chain Store Paradox', *Theory and Decision* 9(2), 127–59.
Sinclair, P. (1987), *Unemployment: Economic Theory and Evidence*, New York: Basil Blackwell.
Trollope, A. (1855–67), *The Chronicles of Barsetshire*, 6 vols, London: Longmans.

11. Do jobs created in CEE countries result in higher productivity?

Michał Gradzewicz

Most of the countries in the world are experiencing a productivity slow-down, for different reasons. With regard to the United States (US), the literature points to almost polar reasons for this phenomenon: the end of the information technology-driven boom of the 1990s (Fernald 2015), or just a drop-off in new business formation and in productivity-enhancing investment by firms (Reifschneider et al. 2015). A common feature of these explanations is that they rely on technology or investments developments, reflecting the fact that basic economic theory says labour productivity is a function of technological progress and capital deepening.

In this chapter, my point of departure is somewhat different: I ask whether an additional person employed has lower than average productivity, thus contributing to a productivity slowdown. To this end I show how the structure of employment has evolved in selected Central and Eastern European (CEE) and euro area (EA) countries, to assess whether the structure evolves in the direction of higher- or lower-productivity jobs.

First, I concentrate on how firms managed to adjust their labour input in terms of extensive and intensive margins. The level of productivity might have been affected by changes in average hours worked. If firms, or households, permanently decide to work more hours, that could be detrimental to productivity. And in fact, average hours worked have been declining. Then, I focus on the evolution of productivity and try to assess the extent of the cyclicality of the productivity slowdown. I will try to show how much of the productivity developments are due to changes in the underlying trend dynamics, and how much can be attributed to changes of the workers' productivity due to cyclical reasons.

As the analysis shows that the slowdown of productivity has a rather long-lasting character, I next focus on structural changes of employment. I discuss the educational structure of employment and the durability of jobs created in recent periods. The underlying observation is that workers with higher education and permanent contracts tend to be more productive due to the higher level of human capital and possible access to training and job-specific human capital investments (e.g., Acemoglu and Autor 2012). Finally, I try to conclude how the developments of real productivity and hours translate into the remuneration of labour input, so I look at the evolution of nominal unit labour cost (ULC). The analysis focuses on selected CEE countries which seem to be quite a representative group (for example, Poland, Hungary, the Czech Republic and Slovakia), but additionally compares them to selected euro zone countries (with diversified labour market developments after 2008, for example Germany and Spain).

11.1　ADJUSTMENTS ON EXTENSIVE AND INTENSIVE MARGINS

Looking into the evolution of the usage of labour input in production processes (see Figure 11.1) in many European countries in the period since the 2008 crisis, one thing clearly emerges: the crisis triggered a decline of average hours worked, whereas the reaction of employment was much more diverse. I will go back to employment evolution in a moment, but one thing to notice is that a clear pattern of labour hoarding emerges in Poland and Germany. In Hungary, the Czech Republic and Slovakia the decline of employment was relatively small and the declining tendency of average hours also suggests some form of labour hoarding in place.

The decline of average hours has been continuing in many countries, despite the increase of employment. It is very visible in the Czech Republic, but also in Germany. The exception is Hungary and – to a certain extent – Poland, where average hours have been increasing since 2013, together with growing employment.

This observation suggests that the usual measures of labour utilization or labour market slack, such as unemployment, may be somewhat misleading. This was observed by Bell and Blanchflower (2013), who introduced an underemployment index for the United Kingdom (UK), which measures the extent of labour utilization simultaneously on the extensive and the intensive margin, using Labour Force Survey (LFS) data on preferred and actually worked hours. Wyszyński (2015) applied this methodology also for Poland, indicating that, initially, a decline of actual hours worked after the crisis was in line with household preferences; whereas after 2010, possibly due to worsening income positions, employees would have wanted to work more than they actually did. Thus, the underutilization of labour was in fact much greater than measured by unemployment alone. The accompanying analysis for Poland shows also that this effect can have a limiting effect on wage growth, as the gap between the supply and demand for hours is bigger than the gap measured by employment alone. The

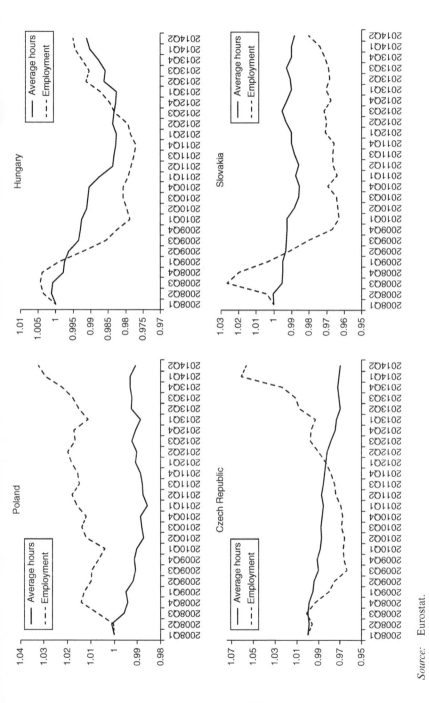

Source: Eurostat.

Figure 11.1 Employment and average hours in selected CEE and EA countries

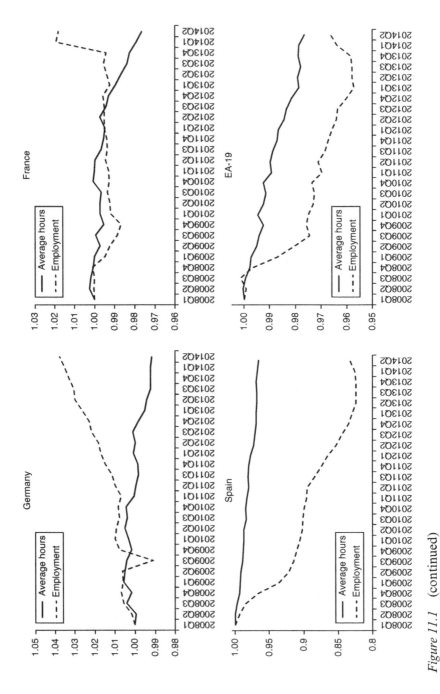

Figure 11.1 (continued)

evolution of hours in other European countries seems to suggest that a similar story applies elsewhere (Blanchflower and Levin 2015, show that this is indeed the case in the US).

11.2 PRODUCTIVITY AND EMPLOYMENT

Having discussed the overall pattern of labour adjustment, I now focus on employment alone and labour productivity. Figure 11.2 shows the evolution of productivity (measured as the annual growth rate of real labour per person productivity) together with the level of employment (measured as LFS employment and normalized to unity in the third quarter of 2008, so in the beginning of the financial crisis).

The first thing to note is that the decline of employment in CEE countries was rather muted (such as in Poland) and limited rather to a relatively short period close to 2009. In Hungary, we observe a continuation of previous declines. In the following years, 2010–2012, employment was flat and started to increase thereafter (again with the exception of Hungary, where it was increasing since 2011). What is more, only Slovakia did not rebuild its pre-crisis level of employment. After 2012 or 2013, the increase of employment in CEE was accompanied by relatively slow growth of real labour productivity, lower than was recorded in the latest employment-growth period before the crisis.

The situation in many euro zone countries was quite similar, but the experiences of euro area countries are more diverse; for example, increases of employment in Germany were accompanied by declines in Spain. But what is common is the behaviour of productivity: it is growing, but at a much slower rate than during the periods before the crisis.

This evidence suggests that limited adjustment of employment in reaction to a crisis, apart from being accompanied by declining average hours worked, resulted in a slowdown of productivity growth. The question arises, then: how much of that slowdown can be indicated as permanent? Moreover, this evidence suggests that the newly created jobs are less productive than the average existing job. So, in consequence, are there any issues in the structure of employment that could suggest it is a permanent feature of the labour market, that we should learn to live with in the future? These are the questions that are addressed in the next sections.

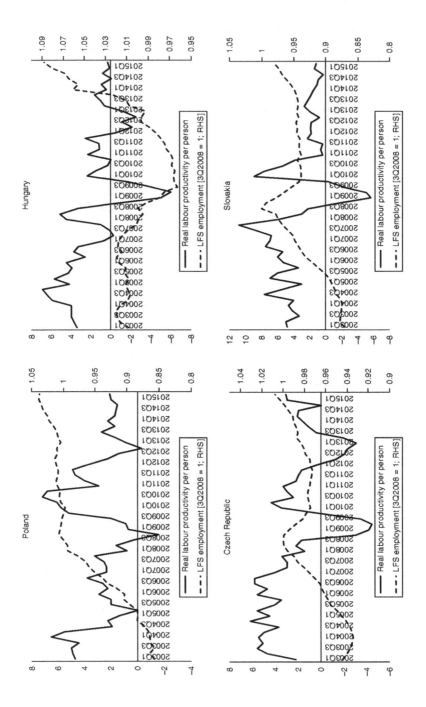

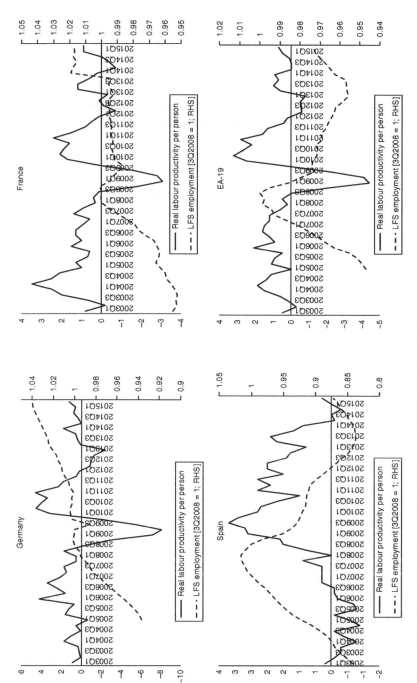

Note: LFS = Labour Force Survey. 3Q = third quarter. RHS = right-hand scale.

Source: Eurostat.

Figure 11.2   Labour productivity and employment in selected CEE and EA countries

11.3 IS THE PRODUCTIVITY SLOWDOWN PERMANENT OR CYCLICAL?

One of the possible ways to assess the extent of cyclicality of productivity is to use spectral methods. Using the fact that the commonly used Hodrick–Prescott filter is actually a high-pass filter and is addictive allows productivity growth to be decomposed into three separate components:

- Trend, defined as fluctuations of periodicity lower than eight years.
- Cycle, defined as fluctuations of periodicity between two and eight years.
- Short-term component, with periodicity higher than two years.

The results of the decomposition are summarized in Figure 11.3 and suggest that the productivity slowdown experienced by many CEE countries could have a different nature:

- It could be a consequence of a slowdown of trend productivity and a close-to-neutral cyclical component, such as in Poland or Slovakia (and to some extent in Spain). The analysis suggests that in the case of these countries the slower growth of productivity could be long-lasting. Even a cyclical economic rebound, when combined with depressed trend productivity, could lead to a limited speed-up of productivity, undermining the real convergence process of these countries.
- It could be a consequence of a relatively stable trend, adjusted by cyclical developments, such as in Hungary and Germany. But in those countries (especially in Hungary) trend productivity growth is so low that the future productivity will probably be flat.

Among the analysed countries, the only optimistic picture emerges for the Czech Republic, where there was indeed a substantial slowdown of productivity growth after the 2008 crisis, but in 2013 the situation reversed and productivity has since been equally driven by trend and by cyclical rebound.

11.4 THE ROLE OF HUMAN CAPITAL

Having said that at least in some countries the productivity slowdown could have been of a more permanent nature, it may be useful to look at the structure of employment and assess whether it points to similar

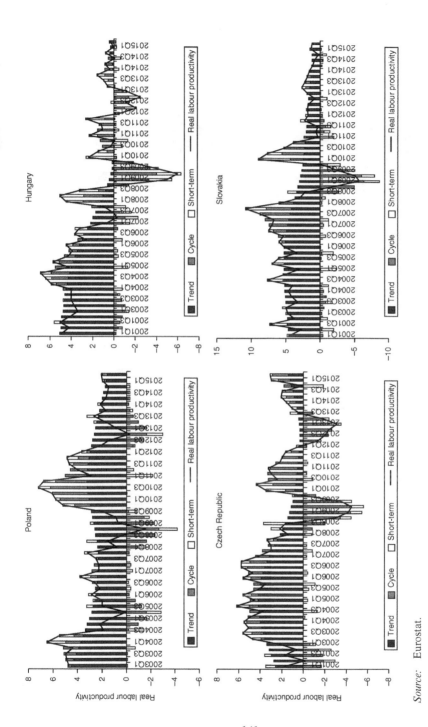

Source: Eurostat.

Figure 11.3 Decomposition of labour productivity of selected CEE and EA countries

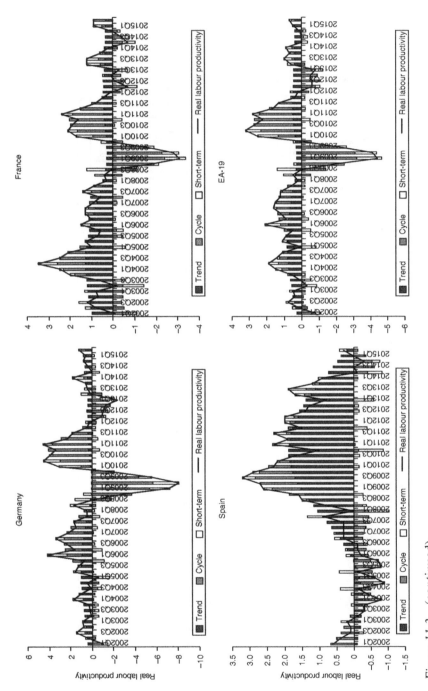

Figure 11.3 (continued)

conclusions. Education is an important ingredient of human capital, and human capital, as the empirical and theoretical literature suggests, is positively related to productivity; so LFS employment growth is decomposed into the growth of employment with primary (levels 0–2 of International Standard Classification of Education (ISCED) 2011), secondary (levels 3–4) and tertiary education (levels 5–8). See Figure 11.4.

This exercise shows that there is a connection between productivity growth and the evolution of the employment educational structure, but it is far from being direct. For example, in Poland, a decline in trend productivity growth during 2004–08 was accompanied by increases of employees with a secondary level of education, and the short-term increase of productivity in 2009–11 with their lay-offs, suggesting a strong connection. But the increases of employment since 2010, in other words in a period of depressed productivity growth, were mainly driven by people with higher education, with simultaneous decreases of groups with a lower level of education. This divergence in Poland could be at least partially explained by the fact that a substantial increase of educational attainment of society was accompanied by a drop in wage premiums on education in remuneration. Gajderowicz et al. (2012) calculated that they declined from c.30 per cent in 1995 to 15 per cent in 2009. The analysis of Narodowy Bank Polski (NBP) points to the same conclusion (BARP 2015).

The story is similar for the Czech Republic, where tertiary education has also been an important aspect of rising employment, in particular since 2013, but in this case it was consistent with rising trend productivity. In Hungary, the employment increase since 2010 is instead observed in the groups of people with primary and secondary education, with a more limited role of tertiary education, which is consistent with the flat profile of trend productivity. The situation is similar in Slovakia, where the decline of trend productivity growth could be linked to the fact that most of the jobs created were mainly for people with lower levels of education.

11.5   THE PERSISTENCE OF JOBS CREATED

Additionally, the impact of education on productivity can be inferred from the type of jobs created: their permanent or temporary nature. Naturally, the more lasting the employee–employment relation, the more likely it is that the human capital of an employee would translate into increased production, leading to a productivity rise.

That factor seems to be a part of the story for the declining trend productivity in Poland and Slovakia (see Figure 11.5). The bulk of the jobs created in these countries are temporary. For Poland, this implies that

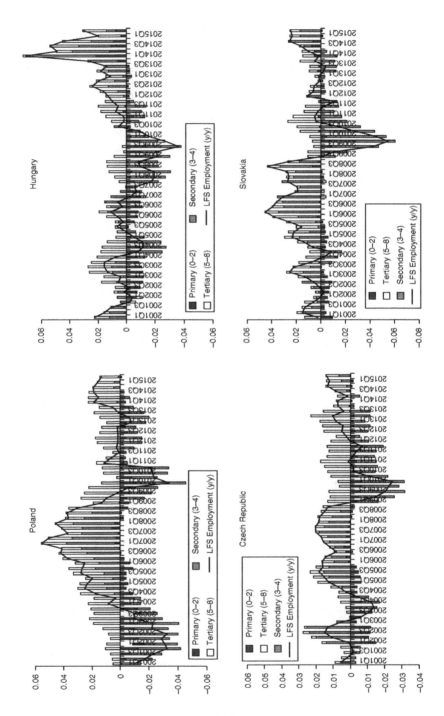

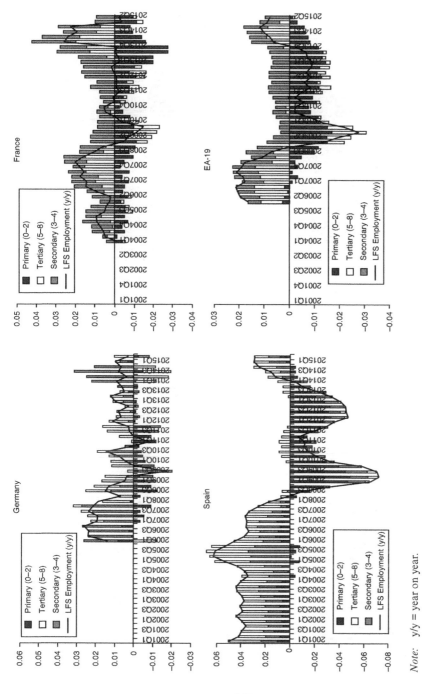

Note: y/y = year on year.

Source: Eurostat, LFS (Labour Force Survey) data.

Figure 11.4 Educational decomposition of LFS employment in selected CEE and EA countries

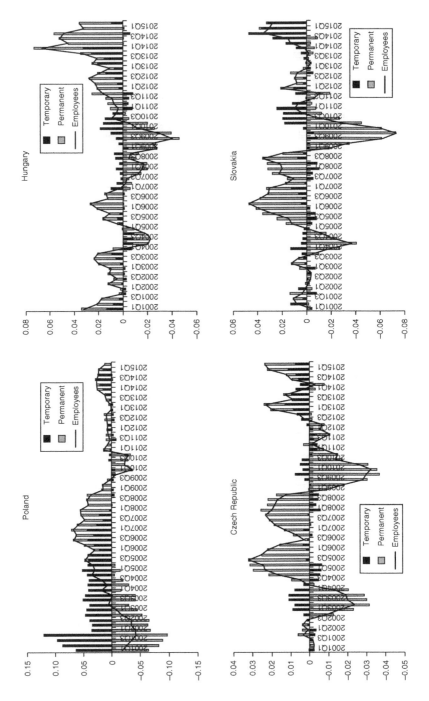

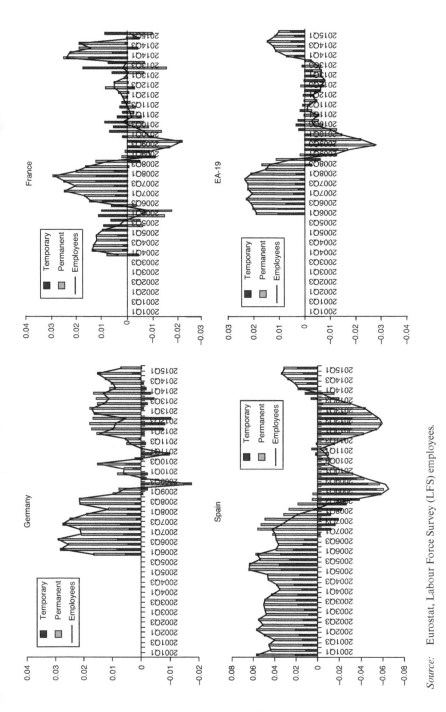

Source: Eurostat, Labour Force Survey (LFS) employees.

Figure 11.5   The role of temporary and permanent contracts in the growth of employees in selected CEE and EA countries

while most jobs created were for people with higher education, these jobs are frequently temporary and thus do not result in substantial productivity increases. In Slovakia, most of the jobs created are for people with secondary education and are temporary, which could explain the sharp slowdown of productivity growth.

In the Czech Republic, the picture is mixed, but both the educational structure and the persistence of jobs created is balanced, possibly not being a hurdle for productivity growth. Only in Hungary was the bulk of employment growth permanent, but at the same time many of those jobs went to people with primary and secondary education, which could explain the flat productivity profile in this country.

11.6 CONCLUSIONS: THE CONSEQUENCES FOR NOMINAL UNIT LABOUR COST

Having discussed the evolution of productivity and the labour market factors that affect its development I turn to the important question of how the labour productivity is being rewarded. I will use nominal unit labour costs as a measure of labour remuneration (see Figure 11.6).

The careful inspection of Figure 11.6 allows the analysed countries to be divided into three distinct groups:

- Countries where the slowing growth of productivity more than offset increases in real wages and, as a consequence, nominal ULC was relatively flat. Poland and Spain are examples of these countries. In Spain the growth of wages was depressed to such an extent that the ULC level was declining until 2013, when it levelled off. This kind of development is favourable to external competitiveness and exports.
- Countries where the productivity level was flat, but real wages were growing, which together resulted in driving up ULC. This kind of development is observed in Hungary, Germany and, to some extent, in the Czech Republic (although here the gap between real productivity and nominal ULC narrowed). Naturally, in these countries the domestic economy is being strengthened as households' disposable incomes are positively affected.
- Relatively similar to the previous group is the case of Slovakia, where ULC was also increasing due to growing real wages, but productivity was also on a growing trend.

The above analysis shows that despite the broad-based slowdown of productivity, its nature and consequences are very diversified. Even

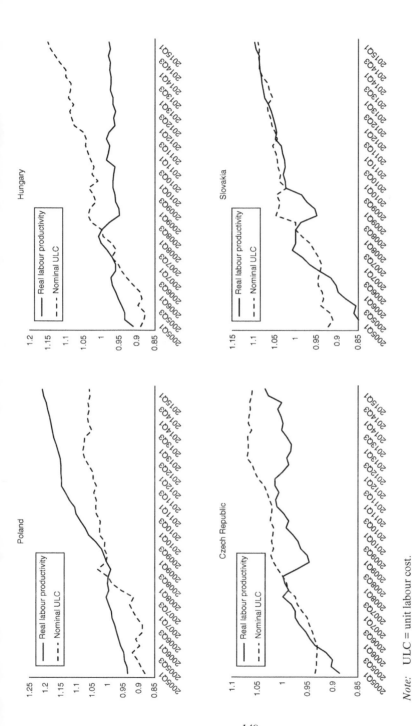

Note: ULC = unit labour cost.

Source: Eurostat, LFS data.

Figure 11.6 Real labour productivity and nominal ULC (both measured in levels, 3Q2008 = 1) in selected CEE and EA countries

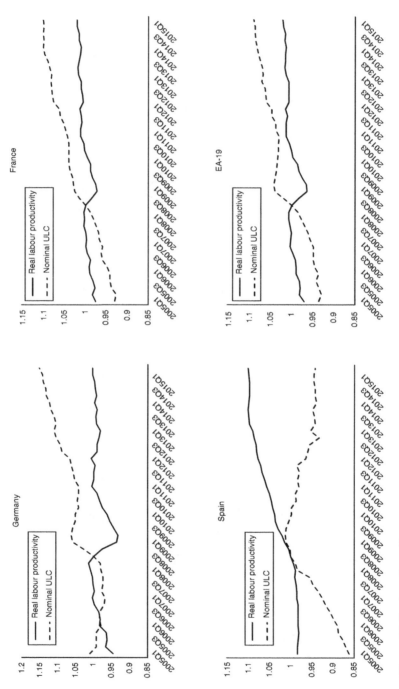

Figure 11.6 (continued)

the development of productivity is different: in Hungary and Germany productivity has not been growing at all since the 2008 crisis, whereas in Poland and Slovakia the productivity growth just slowed down. In the Czech Republic productivity started to increase, and it seems that this growth is permanent. In some countries, such as Poland, productivity slowed down even though new recruits were mostly people with higher education; whereas in Slovakia the bulk of employment growth concerns people with lower levels of education. Also, the remuneration of productivity growth is different in the analysed countries. Remuneration is very poor in Poland and, to some extent, in the Czech Republic; and much more generous in Hungary and, to some extent, in Slovakia. With this level of diversity among CESEE countries, the fact that we observe quite similar developments of employment and wages could mean quite different things for those countries. One should have this pattern in mind when interpreting the current economic developments in these countries.

REFERENCES

Acemoglu, D. and D. Autor (2012), 'What Does Human Capital Do? A Review of Goldin and Katz's "The Race between Education and Technology"', *Journal of Economic Literature* 50(2), 426–63.

BARP (2015), 'Badanie Ankietowe Rynku Pracy 2015' (Labour Market Survey 2015), Economic Institute, Narodowy Bank Polski.

Bell, D.N.F. and D.G. Blanchflower (2013), 'How to Measure Underemployment?', Working Paper WP13-7, Washington, DC: Peterson Institute for International Economics.

Blanchflower, D.G. and A.T. Levin (2015), 'Labor Market Slack and Monetary Policy', NBER Working Papers 21094, Cambridge, MA: National Bureau of Economic Research.

Fernald, J.G. (2015), 'Productivity and Potential Output Before, During, and After the Great Recession', in J. Parker and M. Woodford (eds), NBER *Macroeconomics Annual 2014*, 29, 1–51.

Gajderowicz, T., G. Grotkowska and L. Wincenciak (2012), 'Premia płacowa z wykształcenia wyższego według grup zawodów' (Wage premium on education for different professions), *Ekonomista* 5, 577–603.

Reifschneider D., W. Wascher and D. Wilcox (2015), 'Aggregate Supply in the United States: Recent Developments and Implications for the Conduct of Monetary Policy', *IMF Economic Review* 63(1), 71–109.

Wyszyński, R. (2015), 'Underemployment index for Poland', unpublished manuscript.

12. Productivity and competitiveness in CESEE countries: a look at the key structural drivers

Dan Andrews and Alain de Serres

Following a period of fairly rapid catching-up vis-à-vis leading countries in the 1990s and early 2000s, the process of economic convergence pursued by many Central, Eastern and South-Eastern European (CESEE) countries has, but for a few exceptions, basically stalled.[1] The failure to maintain a growth pace sufficiently strong to close significant income gaps is owed primarily to a slowdown in productivity, although the limited progress in raising the very low employment rates observed in some of the countries has not helped. Resuming catching-up will require a significant boost to productivity growth. And, given the magnitude of the gap in average productivity levels vis-à-vis most advanced economies, future productivity growth in CESEE countries will largely depend on the capacity of domestic firms to harness the force of knowledge diffusion from firms operating at the frontier; essentially large multinational enterprises.

One way to measure the effectiveness of knowledge diffusion is to assess the extent to which productivity gains at the frontier spill over or translate into higher productivity among domestic firms, and at what speed. Some of the key factors shaping this effectiveness include global connections (cross-border trade and investment), investment in knowledge-based capital, and the efficiency with which the resources are allocated across firms and industries. These drivers are in turn influenced by a number of structural policy settings, the most important of which include pro-competition reforms, with a particular attention on firm entry and exit, but also policies promoting the collaboration between firms and universities (so that basic research can more easily benefit non-frontier firms), policies that provide better access to early-stage venture capital as well as those facilitating the mobility of labour, and a good matching between skills and job tasks.

The purpose of this chapter is to provide an international perspective on the performance of CESEE countries as the key drivers of knowledge diffusion and productivity, and to identify the related policy areas where the scope for improving outcomes is largest. The chapter starts with a brief overview of the productivity performance since the 1990s, followed by an examination of how well CESEE countries appear to be integrated in global trade flows. Going beyond trade openness, the chapter then examines how much investment is made in these countries to boost innovation, and the extent to which the return on innovation efforts is potentially hampered by a relatively inefficient allocation of labour resources across firms. The chapter closes with a review of the policy priorities to promote the diffusion of technology and knowledge among domestic firms and to raise their incentives and capacity to make the most of productivity gains at the frontier.

12.1   A SHARP SLOWDOWN IN PRODUCTIVITY AFTER THE CRISIS

CESEE countries are still lagging more advanced economies in terms of living standards, but with substantial variations across countries (as well as across regions within countries). The gap in gross domestic product (GDP) per capita vis-à-vis the upper half of Organisation of Economic Co-operation and Development (OECD) countries varies from 60 per cent in Turkey to around 40 per cent for Slovenia (OECD 2015a). In most cases, virtually all of this income gap is accounted for by a shortfall in average labour productivity, that is, the output produced per unit of labour. This is not to suggest that there are no issues related to labour market outcomes. Higher employment rates would also contribute to raising GDP per capita, but with the exception of Turkey and, to a much lesser extent, the Slovak Republic and Slovenia, the performance of CESEE countries in terms of total hours worked relative to the working-age population is broadly comparable to that observed in advanced economies. Productivity is thus the main channel through which structural reforms can durably lift growth.

One worrying global development about productivity has been the widespread deceleration since the crisis (Figure 12.1). In the case of most advanced economies, the slowdown precedes the crisis and even goes back to the early 2000s, raising concerns that deeper structural weaknesses lie behind the trend. Adding to these concerns is the fact that the downward trend has been accompanied by a slowdown in the accumulation of knowledge-based capital between the 1990s and the 2000s, as well as by a decline in the pace of business start-ups, both factors being important underlying contributors to the stronger productivity gains of the 1990s.

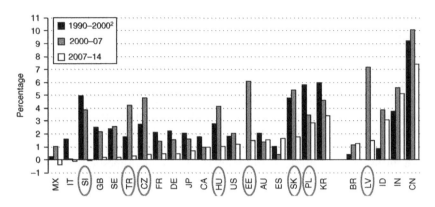

Notes:
1. GDP per employee for non-OECD countries.
2. For Brazil, Hungary, Indonesia and Mexico, the data refer to 1991–2000. For the Czech Republic and Poland, the data refer to 1993–2000. For the Slovak Republic and Slovenia, the data refer to 1995–2000.

Source: OECD, National Accounts and Productivity Databases; International Labour Organization (ILO) Database.

Figure 12.1   *Productivity slowed sharply in most CESEE countries;*
                average annual growth rate of GDP per hour worked[1]

CESEE countries have not escaped the deceleration, but one major difference is that in their case, the slowdown began with the crisis, not much before. As a result, the decline in growth was more brutal, falling to near zero in Slovenia, Turkey and the Czech Republic; but its timing leaves somewhat better hopes of a stronger cyclical component. Indeed, one of the factors contributing to the labour productivity slowdown is the persistent weakness in investment in tangible or physical capital (building, machines and equipment) since the crisis. A look at the current levels of real GDP and investment relative to their pre-crisis levels illustrates the extent to which investment is lagging GDP, with the lag being particularly severe across most of Europe (Figure 12.2).

For example, while GDP has basically returned to its pre-crisis level in the Czech Republic, Estonia, the Slovak Republic and Hungary, investment remains around 10 per cent below the pre-crisis level. In Slovenia, this figure is 35 per cent. The situation in the latter is similar to the case of Southern European countries that have been hit hardest by the crisis (Greece, Italy, Portugal and Spain), where the investment lag reflects both the collapse of public investment under the pressures from fiscal consolidation as well as the impact of post-crisis private sector deleveraging.

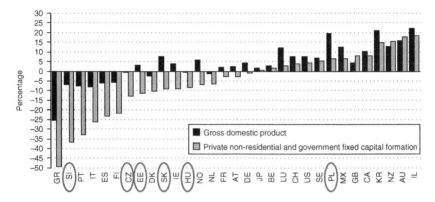

Note: Data for investment refer to 2013 for Switzerland, Hungary, Ireland and Poland; 2012 for Mexico.

Source: OECD, Economic Outlook Database.

Figure 12.2   Investment is lagging GDP. Difference between 2014 and 2008 levels, percentage of the 2008 level

Among CESEE countries, Poland stands out for the relative strength of GDP growth throughout and after the crisis, but even there investment has lagged.

Clearly a pick-up in investment will help to boost productivity growth in CESEE countries, but considering the magnitude of the productivity gap vis-à-vis advanced economies, far more than a recovery in the pace of tangible capital accumulation will be needed to pursue convergence and maintain competitiveness, let alone improve it. In fact, for countries with a sizeable gap in productivity, and which still have considerable scope for growth through the adoption and adaptation of technologies and knowledge developed elsewhere, stronger productivity will largely be influenced by the ability of domestic firms to make the most of knowledge diffusion.

Recent OECD research has allowed for the identification of a number of factors having a strong influence on the diffusion of know-how and technology and thus productivity gains from frontier firms to lagging ones (Saia et al. 2015; Andrews et al. 2015). These include: (1) global connectedness through trade intensity and participation in global value chains; (2) investment in innovation and knowledge-based capital; and (3) respective areas in comparison to advanced economies, all of which are examined in the next sections.

12.2   THE ROLE OF CROSS-BORDER TRADE IN CESEE PRODUCTIVITY PERFORMANCE

International trade and investment play a critical role in the ability of firms to learn from the frontier and sustain productivity growth. Trade and foreign direct investment (FDI) boost productivity through multiple channels including: (1) stronger competition, thus encouraging more efficient use of inputs and stimulating innovation; (2) greater scope for exploiting increasing returns to scale through bigger markets without adversely affecting the intensity of competition; (3) faster diffusion of technology through trade in goods and participation in global value chains (GVCs); (4) diffusion of managerial best practice and know-how through FDI and the presence of multinationals. The latter two channels will hinge in particular on the degree of connectedness with countries that are at the global frontier in trade goods and services or investment areas.

Trade is one area where for the most part CESEE countries are doing comparatively well, as can be seen from Figure 12.3, which shows the intensity of external trade against the size of the country. The reason for controlling for size is that smaller countries are expected to be naturally more open, so as to access markets with sufficient size and have access to the same variety of products that larger countries can achieve. In the figure,

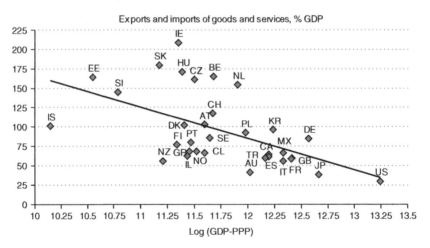

Note: Log (GDP-PPP) = logarithm of gross domestic product at purchasing power parity.

Source: OECD, Economic Outlook Database.

Figure 12.3   CESEE countries benefit from high cross-border trade intensity, 2014

the intensity of trade is thus measured by the distance to the regression line. Countries that are close to or on the regression line have similar degrees of openness to trade. On that measure, the Czech Republic, Hungary and the Slovak Republic figure among the group of most open countries in the OECD, along with Ireland, Belgium and the Netherlands. Considering the size of its domestic economy, trade openness in Poland is slightly above average, albeit below that observed in Korea, while Turkey would benefit from exposing its economy to stronger cross-border exchanges.

Although trade plays a key role in facilitating learning from the frontier (Alvarez et al. 2013), geographical distance remains an important obstacle to sharing knowledge given its essentially tacit and non-codifiable characteristic and the local nature of spillovers. This is true for embodied and even more so for disembodied knowledge transfers (Keller and Yeaple 2013). In this regard, one factor contributing to the relatively strong trade intensity among CESEE countries is the proximity to major and well-developed markets. Extending a methodology developed in Redding and Venables (2004), Boulhol and de Serres (2010) computed a measure of access to market and suppliers for OECD countries, which was later extended in de Serres et al. (2014). Beyond distance, the measure takes into account that the size, growth and degree of openness of foreign markets also matter in determining the scope of trade opportunities.

Based on this measure, Belgium and the Netherlands have the most privileged access to a large market while, unsurprisingly, Australia and New Zealand suffer from the biggest geographical handicap among OECD countries (Figure 12.4). Small CESEE countries generally benefit from a relatively favourable market and some of them have fully taken advantage of this proximity to be well-integrated in GVCs. As shown in Figure 12.4, the participation in GVCs of firms from the Czech Republic, Hungary and the Slovak Republic is significantly stronger than in many other countries (including Austria, Belgium and the Netherlands) that benefit from similar or even more favourable access to large markets.

GVCs comprise a wide range of value creation, from the development of a new concept to basic research, product design, supply of core material or components, assembly into final goods, distribution, retail, after-sales service and marketing (including branding). Participating in these segments of a GVC enables firms to capture world demand without having to develop a whole supply chain and full set of underlying capabilities. From an economy-wide perspective, this means that countries can exert export competitiveness in specific GVC activities without building up a full set of supporting industries. The strong participation of several CESEE countries has certainly contributed to the productivity catching-up. However, their manufacturing exports still embody a relatively small share of domestic value

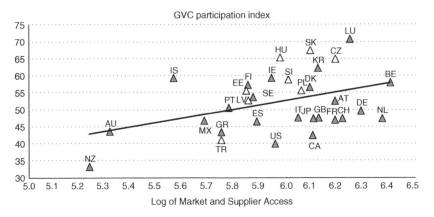

Sources: OECD Trade in Value Added (TiVA) database and de Serres et al. (2014).

*Figure 12.4   Integration into global value chains is associated with a good
              access to large markets; index of market and supplier access
              and GVC participation, 2011*

added arising from services, where the value added created by GVCs is often
concentrated. Moving up the value chain requires stronger capabilities in
knowledge and skill-intensive activities within GVCs (such as new product
development, manufacturing of core components, or brand development).

12.3   THE CONTRIBUTION OF INNOVATION AND KNOWLEDGE-BASED CAPITAL

Openness to trade and FDI is a fundamental driver of productivity through
diffusion of knowledge and technology but is not sufficient to move up the
value chain. Complementary investments in research and development
(R&D), skills, organizational know-how (managerial quality) and other
forms of so-called knowledge-based capital are necessary to enable economies to absorb, adapt and reap the full benefits of new technologies. Some
aspects of new technologies are difficult to codify and require practical
investigation before they can be properly incorporated into production
processes, and hence the availability of researchers who can demystify
'tacit' knowledge plays a crucial role. In this regard, a strong domestic
R&D sector is important for countries' ability to benefit from new dis-
coveries by facilitating the adoption of foreign technologies (Griffith
et al. 2004). Moreover, implementing and realizing the full productivity
benefits from new technologies (such as information and communication

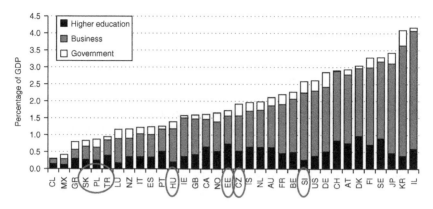

Note: For Australia (Higher education and Government), Switzerland and Ireland (for Business only), the data refer to 2012. For Australia (Business) and for Mexico the data refer to 2011.

Source: OECD, Main Science and Technology Indicators Database.

Figure 12.5   *Spending on R&D varies substantially across CESEE countries; R&D as % of GDP, 2013*

technologies, ICTs) entails significant organizational restructuring, which requires considerable managerial skill (Bloom et al. 2012).

Enormous progress has been made in measuring investment in key components of knowledge-based capital, but finding comparable data covering a large set of countries remains difficult. One exception is R&D, which can be taken as a rough indication of countries' efforts in investment in complementary components. Not surprisingly, CESEE countries are generally lagging advanced economies in this area, except for Estonia and the Czech Republic where R&D spending as a percentage of GDP is close to the OECD average of 2 per cent, and Slovenia where it is even above (Figure 12.5). One factor contributing to the higher spending on R&D by businesses in Hungary and Slovenia is the relatively generous financial support provided by the state through tax credits and, especially, direct government funding in the form of research grants.

Data from the European Union Community Innovation Survey show that firms performing R&D are more likely to bring new product or process to the market than firms without R&D – which in itself is not surprising – but also that the difference in the innovation performance between the two types of firms is particularly large in CESEE countries (OECD 2015b). This suggests that for various reasons performing R&D makes a bigger difference in these countries. At the same time, since the proportion of firms that are R&D-active is relatively small, raising the propensity of non-R&D firms to innovate could also significantly boost these countries' overall innovation performance. The point is not that each of these countries should try to turn themselves into large producers of high-tech product, but more whether they make the necessary investment – not just in R&D but in knowledge-based capital in general – to be able to use ICT and new technologies in a way to develop high-quality services.

One indicator of such capacity to leverage the potential of ICT is a measure of the readiness and usage among the population, businesses and governments. In short, it provides a survey-based indication of the extent of connectedness. As shown in Figure 12.6, CESEE countries are more uniformly lagging in this area, ranking between Greece and Spain. This indicates the importance of improving ICT infrastructure and related regulatory frameworks. For instance, the number of fixed (wired) broadband subscriptions per population is well below the OECD average in Turkey, Poland, the Czech Republic and the Slovak Republic, and closer to average – albeit below Greece and Spain – in Estonia, Slovenia and

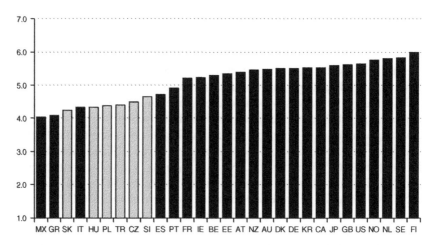

Note: The Networked Readiness Index is published in the Global Information Technology Report series, prepared by the World Economic Forum's Global Competitiveness and Risks Team and the Industry Partnership Programme for Information and Communication Technologies, in collaboration with the graduate business school INSEAD and with Cornell University as of 2014.

Source: World Economic Forum, the Global Information Technology Report 2015.

Figure 12.6   ICT readiness and usage among population, businesses and governments is relatively low; index scale: 1 (lowest) to 7 (highest), 2015

Hungary (OECD 2015c). Several factors can contribute to the gap, but the efficiency and competitiveness of the telecom sector most certainly plays a key role. The OECD indicator of product market regulation suggests that the performance of this sector could be fostered by lowering regulatory barriers to entry and competition, which are relatively high compared to other OECD countries (Koske et al. 2015).

12.4   THE EFFICENCY OF RESOURCE ALLOCATION

Making the most of investment in innovation and ICT also requires that resources in labour and capital be able to flow smoothly across firms and sectors. The efficient reallocation of scarce resources is particularly important to allow the most innovative firms to reach a sufficient scale to fully recover fixed costs of research and entry into global markets, but also to fulfil the high growth potential that comes with the commercialization of successful ideas. In catching-up countries, an economy's potential to adopt frontier innovations will also depend on its ability to reallocate resources to the most productive firms (Andrews and Criscuolo 2013). The large dispersion in firm productivity performance that is observed even within narrowly defined sectors contributes to pull down aggregate productivity (Syverson 2011). The latter could be lower than otherwise due to a technological gap that national firms face relative to the global frontier, or to a weak market selection process enabling too many bad performers to survive in the market, or both.

One way to assess the efficiency of resource allocation in the economy is to measure the extent to which the most productive firms in an industry are also the ones with the largest market share. Considering the surprisingly large degree of heterogeneity in the productivity level of firms within an industry, one would expect the most productive firms to grow more rapidly and the least productive to shrink or even exit, at least in a well-performing economy. One measure of allocative efficiency consists in looking at the difference between the aggregate level of productivity observed in a given sector, and the level that would be obtained if labour resources were equally distributed between high- and low-productivity firms across the sector.[2] The more the actual allocation of resources is skewed towards high-productivity firms, the higher the difference will be between the two measures of aggregate productivity.

Based on this measure, Figure 12.7 shows the contribution of the allocation of employment to the average level of productivity in the business sector across a number of country groups in comparison to the United States. The results indicate that in the United States and Nordic countries,

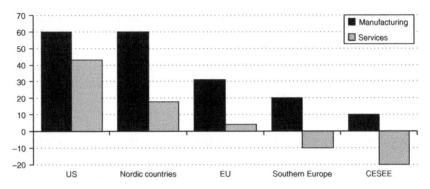

Source: Andrews and Cingano (2014).

Figure 12.7 *The scope for productivity gains through better resource
allocation is substantial; contribution of the allocation of
employment across firms to the level of labour productivity,
%, late 2000s*

aggregate productivity in the manufacturing sector is around 60 per cent
higher than it would be if employees were equally distributed across firms,
reflecting a relatively efficient allocation of resources. Efficient resource
allocation is more difficult to achieve in services, where the numbers suggest
a productivity premium of around 40 per cent and 20 per cent in the United
States and Nordic countries, respectively. As one moves from Northern
Europe to Southern and Central Europe, one finds a much lower contribution of resource allocation to productivity, which even turns negative in the
case of services. The scope for productivity gains through resource reallocation is therefore quite high in these countries, unless cross-firm differences
in productivity essentially reflect differences in the workers' skills.

In this regard, the mismatch between the skills of workers and those that
are required for the job is another aspect to the misallocation of resources.
Recent analysis based on the Programme for the International Assessment
of Adult Competencies (PIAAC) survey of adult skills and competencies
shows that in industries with higher rates of overskilling, more-productive
firms have lower employment shares than otherwise would be, which
lowers aggregate productivity (McGowan and Andrews 2015). Indeed,
high rates of skills mismatch often coincide with the presence of many
small and old firms. One possible explanation is that as firms draw from a
scarce and fixed pool of skilled labour, trapping resources in relatively low-
productivity firms – which tends to occur in industries with a high share
of overskilled workers – can make it more difficult for more-productive
firms to attract skilled labour and gain market share at the expense of

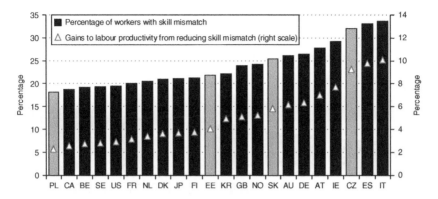

Note: The figure shows the percentage of workers who are either over- or underskilled and the simulated gains to allocative efficiency from reducing skill mismatch in each country to the best practice level of mismatch. The figures are based on OECD calculations using OECD, Survey of Adult Skills, 2012.

Source: McGowan and Andrews (2015).

Figure 12.8   *The mismatch of skills and jobs requirements also acts as a constraint on productivity; % of workers with skill mismatch and implied gain in productivity from reducing mismatch, selected OECD countries, 2011–12*

less-productive firms. This can be particularly damaging to the growth prospects of young innovative firms (Acemoglu et al. 2013).

The data from the PIAAC survey show that on average across countries, roughly one-quarter of workers report a mismatch between their existing skills and those required for their job – that is, either they are overskilled or underskilled; but this figure is closer to one-third in Italy, Spain and the Czech Republic (Figure 12.8). Among other CESEE countries covered, the extent of skills mismatch is also found to be high in the Slovak Republic, but much less so in Estonia and especially Poland. The empirical analysis reported in McGowan and Andrews (2015) suggests that a better use of skills in Italy, Spain and the Czech Republic could boost the level of labour productivity by up to 10 per cent, as also shown in Figure 12.8. This underscores the likelihood that the productivity differential across firms reflects not so much a difference in the skills level of workers, but rather a difference in the ability of management to best match the skills potential of employees with technology. In such a case, the potential gains in aggregate productivity gains from reallocating workers from low- to high-productivity firms are less likely to be offset by a reduction in the productivity level within the firms that are absorbing new workers.

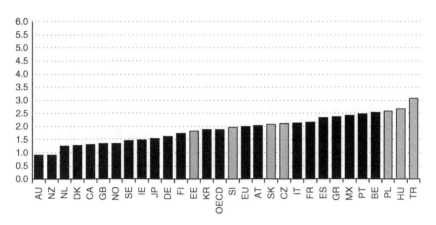

Source: OECD Product market regulation database.

*Figure 12.9   Regulatory barriers to firm entry are relatively high;
                administrative burden on start-ups, index scale: 0–6 from least
                to most restrictive*

Improving the efficiency of resource allocation requires that regulatory
barriers to firm entry and exit be lowered so as to allow for new innovative
firms to enter the market and challenge incumbents, encouraging them
to innovate as a means to escape competition. The scope for lowering
regulatory barriers to entry in CESEE countries is relatively large, as indicated by the OECD indicator of product market regulation which shows
particularly high administrative burden on start-ups in Poland, Hungary
and Turkey, and to a lesser extent in the Czech Republic and Slovenia
(Figure 12.9). Furthermore, bankruptcy legislation needs to be designed in
a way to avoid overpenalizing business failure, so as to encourage entrepre-
neurship and experimentation. It must also facilitate the exit of non-viable
firms to avoid limiting the capacity of young innovative firms to rapidly
scale up production and get the most of the high growth potential from
new ideas. One indicator of the efficiency of bankruptcy legislation shows
that CESEE countries lag most other OECD countries in terms of the cost
of exit procedures (Figure 12.10).

The efficiency of resource allocation would be further increased by
reforms that reduce barriers to labour mobility and skills mismatch. This
includes reforms of housing market policies that create high transaction
costs, restricted housing supply or rigid rental markets; as well as of adult
learning and vocational education programmes to raise the focus on skills
complementarity with technical progress and the ease of adaptation to
rapid changes in the nature of tasks. Reforming housing market policies

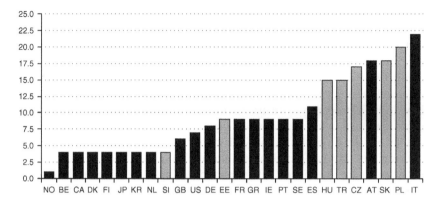

Source: World Bank Doing Business Database.

Figure 12.10 Efficient firm exit procedures are also important for good resource allocations; cost of bankruptcy procedures, % of estate

is identified as a priority to improve employment and growth in Poland and the Slovak Republic, while improving the availability and effectiveness of lifelong learning and job-related training is a priority in the Czech Republic, Poland, the Slovak Republic, Slovenia and Turkey (OECD 2015a).

12.5 SUMMARY

This chapter has reviewed the comparative performance of CESEE countries with respect to three drivers of productivity that have been found to play a key role in the diffusion of knowledge and technology from frontier sectors or firms to lagging ones: (1) the degree of trade openness and the participation in global value chains; (2) the intensity of investment in knowledge-based capital; and (3) the efficiency of resource allocation. CESEE countries are found to be generally well connected in global trade flows and well integrated in global value chains, with the exception of Turkey and, to a lesser extent, Poland.

The performance in terms of investment in knowledge-based capital and innovation activities is more mixed. Business spending on R&D is relatively high in Slovenia, Estonia and the Czech Republic, but most CESEE countries are well below the OECD average in terms of ICT readiness and usage among the population, businesses and governments. This underscores the importance of improving ICT infrastructure, in particular with respect to high-speed networks, and in some cases of reviewing the regulatory framework to boost competition and efficiency in the telecom sector.

The efficiency of resource allocation is one area where a huge gap in the performance of CESEE countries vis-à-vis best-performing OECD countries is found. Large gains in economy-wide productivity could be achieved through the reallocation of labour and capital resources from low- to high-productivity firms. An inefficient allocation of resources and weak reallocation are indicative of high barriers to firm entry and exit as well as of friction in the mobility of labour resources across firms, sectors and regions. Lowering regulatory barriers to competition to boost firm entry, reducing the cost of bankruptcy procedures to facilitate the exit of non-viable firms, as well as improving adult learning and vocational education programmes while easing housing market-related frictions to labour mobility, should be on the reform agenda of most CESEE countries.

NOTES

1. This chapter focuses on the CESEE countries that are members of the OECD (Czech Republic, Estonia, Hungary, Latvia, Poland, Slovak Republic, Slovenia and Turkey) as well as Latvia, which is in the process of accession.
2. The measure is based on the cross-sectional industry level decomposition of productivity developed in Olley and Pakes (1996) and applied to a large set of OECD countries on the basis of Orbis data by Andrews and Cingano (2014).

REFERENCES

Acemoglu, D., U. Akcigit, N. Bloom and W. Kerr (2013), 'Innovation, Reallocation and Growth', NBER Working Papers, No. 18993.

Alvarez, F., F. Buera and R. Lucas, Jr (2013), 'Idea Flows, Economic Growth and Trade', NBER Working Paper Series, No. 19667.

Andrews, D. and F. Cingano (2014), 'Public Policy and Resource Allocation: Evidence from Firms in OECD Countries', *Economic Policy* 29(78), 253–96.

Andrews, D. and C. Criscuolo (2013), 'Knowledge Based Capital, Innovation and Resource Allocation', OECD Economics Department Working Papers, No. 1046, OECD Publishing.

Andrews, D., C. Criscuolo and P. Gal (2015), 'Frontier Firms, Technology Diffusion and Public Policy: Micro Evidence from OECD Countries', OECD Productivity Working Papers No 2, OECD Publishing.

Bloom, N., R. Sadun and J. Van Reenen (2012), 'Americans Do IT Better: US Multinationals and the Productivity Miracle', *American Economic Review* 102(1), 167–201.

Boulhol, H. and A. de Serres (2010), 'Have Developed Countries Escaped the Curse of Distance?', *Journal of Economic Geography* 10(1), 113–39.

De Serres, A., N. Yashiro and H. Boulhol (2014), 'An International Perspective on the New Zealand Productivity Paradox', New Zealand Productivity Commission Working Paper No. 2014/01.

Griffith, R., S. Redding and J. Van Reenen (2004), 'Mapping the Two Faces of R&D: Productivity Growth in a Panel of OECD Industries', *Review of Economics and Statistics* 86(4), 883–95.

Keller, W. and S. Yeaple (2013), 'The Gravity of Knowledge', *American Economic Review* 103(4), 1414–44.

Koske, I., I. Wanner, R. Bitetti and O. Barbiero (2015), 'The 2013 Update Of The OECD Product Market Regulation Indicators: Policy Insights For OECD And Non-OECD Countries', OECD Economics Department Working Papers, 1200/2015, Paris: OEC Publishing.

McGowan, M.A. and D. Andrews (2015), 'Labour Market Mismatch and Labour Productivity: Evidence from PIAAC Data', OECD Economics Department Working Papers, No. 1209, Paris: OECD Publishing.

OECD (2015a), 'OECD 2015 Going for Growth', Paris: OECD Publishing.

OECD (2015b), 'OECD Science, Technology and Industry Scoreboard 2015', Paris: OECD Publishing.

OECD (2015c), 'OECD Digital Economy Outlook 2015', Paris: OECD Publishing.

Olley, G.S. and A. Pakes (1996), 'The Dynamics of Productivity in the Telecommunications Equipment Industry', *Econometrica* 64(6), 1263–97.

Redding, S. and A.J. Venables (2004), 'Economic Geography and International Inequality', *Journal of International Economics* 62(1), 53–82.

Saia, A., D. Andrews and S. Albrizio (2015), 'Productivity spill-overs from the global frontier and public policy: industry level evidence', OECD Economics Department Working Papers No. 1238, Paris: OECD Publishing.

Syverson, C. (2011), 'What Determines Productivity?', *Journal of Economic Literature* 49(2), 326–65.

PART V

CESEE's contribution to growth in the euro area and Europe

13. Convergence of 'new' EU member states: past, present and future

Bas B. Bakker and Krzysztof Krogulski*

The convergence and integration of Central and Eastern European (CEE) economies with the European Union (EU) is undoubtedly one of Europe's success stories. In 2014 the tenth anniversary of the first EU enlargement to the east was celebrated. Currently, 11 formerly communist CEE countries are members of the European Union; they have all narrowed the income gap with Western Europe. However, continued convergence may be more challenging as the 'low-hanging fruit' has been picked. Productivity and employment are no longer very low, while unfavourable demographics will provide strong headwinds.

13.1 CONVERGENCE: PAST AND PRESENT

As is well known, income levels in CEE were converging rapidly with those in Western Europe in the pre-crisis years (Figure 13.1, left panel). Between 2000 and 2007, gross domestic product (GDP) per capita in CEE grew by almost 6 per cent annually, compared with only 1.5 per cent in the EU15. There were differences in growth among the various subregions, with the most rapid growth in the Baltics, and the weakest in non-EU South-Eastern Europe (SEE), but growth in all subregions[1] was strong.

What may be less well known is that convergence has continued post-crisis (Figure 13.1, right panel). Much of CEE went through a deep crisis in 2009, as the capital inflows-fuelled domestic demand boom came to a sudden end. As a result of the deep recession, growth in CEE over the 2008–15 period was much weaker than during the boom years. Indeed, during 2008–15, GDP growth per capita in CEE averaged only 1.5 per cent. However, this was still better than Western Europe: GDP per capita growth in the EU15 during 2008–15 was negative. Thus, by 2015, the gap in income per capita between CEE and the EU15 was smaller than it was in 2008. Slovenia and Croatia were notable exceptions; their income gap widened post-2008.

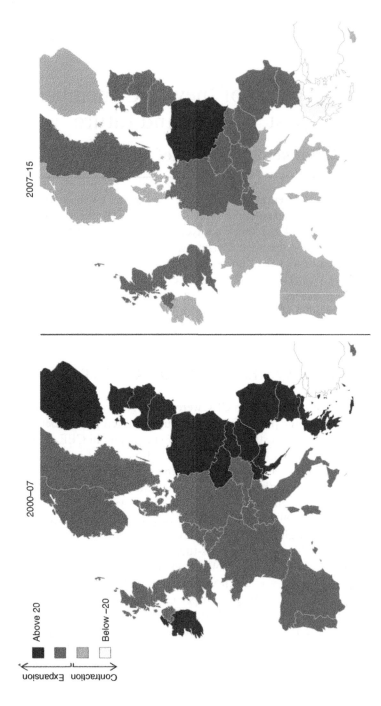

Sources: AMECO ('Annual macro-economic') database of the European Commission and authors' calculations.

Figure 13.1   Real GDP per capita growth in Europe (%)

As a result of the income convergence, there is no longer a clear divide in income levels between east and west (Figure 13.2). At the turn of the millennium, Western Europe was rich, and Eastern Europe poor. In 2015, there is no longer a clear divide. There is now a rich centre, which stretches from the Netherlands in the north, to the northern part of Italy in the south. Regions to both the west and to the east of the centre are poorer. Eastern Europe is no longer uniformly poor: the Mazowieckie region in Poland now has an income level above the EU average, and well above that of most of France. South-Eastern Europe remains relatively poor, but overall there has been tremendous convergence.

13.2   THE NEW MEMBER STATES: AN IMPORTANT SOURCE OF DEMAND

The 'new' EU member states are an important contributor to EU growth (Figure 13.3). In 2014–15, their share in the EU28's GDP growth was one-quarter, even though their share in EU28's GDP is only one-eighth. Seen over a longer time period, their contribution is even larger: despite accounting for just 11 per cent of today's EU28 GDP in 2004, the new member states added some one-third of EU GDP growth in the period 2004–15, and this ratio does not appear to have changed after the crisis.

The 'new' EU member states are also an important export market for Western Europe: currently they account for about 10 per cent of the euro zone's exports. Interestingly, the share of imports by the EU's 'new' member states in Western Europe's exports is now higher than it was in 2007, even though current account deficits in CEE have declined sharply post-crisis (Figure 13.4).

13.3   THE 'NEW' MEMBER STATES: AN IMPORTANT SOURCE OF EU LABOUR

Large wage differentials have contributed to large-scale emigration of labour from east to west. It is estimated that by 2012 some 4 million people had emigrated from CEE to other EU countries. The pre-crisis booms in the construction sector provided many new jobs for foreigners, even those with weak foreign language skills. Post-crisis, immigration patterns have changed, with Spain and Ireland now seeing labour outflows; but countries where the labour market has held up better have seen continued inflows (Figure 13.5).

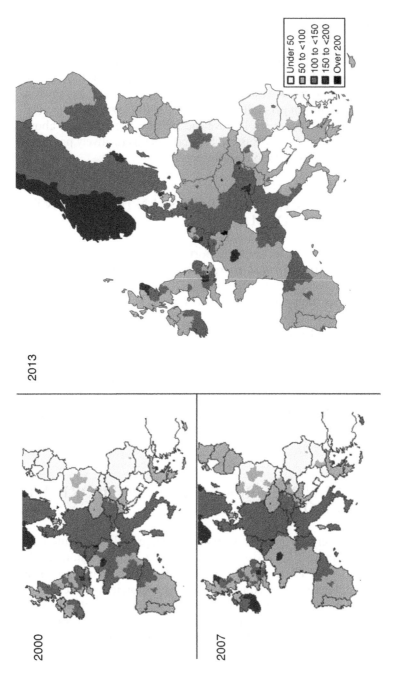

2013

2000

2007

Under 50
50 to <100
100 to <150
150 to <200
Over 200

Sources: Eurostat and authors' calculations.

Figure 13.2   GDP per capita (% of the EU average)

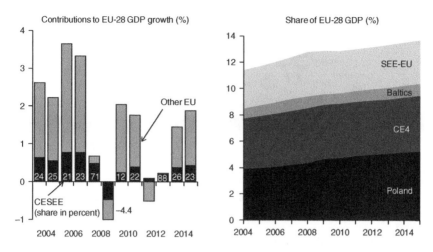

Sources: WEO (World Economic Outlook) database of the IMF and authors' calculations.

Figure 13.3 Contributions to EU GDP and real GDP growth (%)

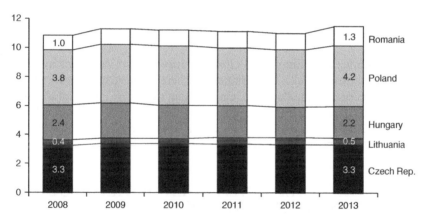

Sources: Eurostat and authors' calculations.

Figure 13.4 Share of euro area exports of goods and services going to 'new' EU member states (%)

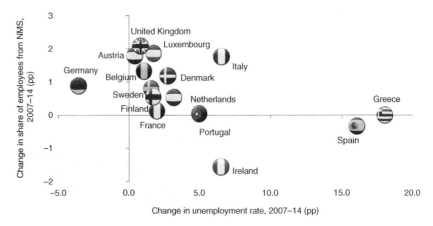

Sources: Eurostat and authors' calculations.

Figure 13.5 Labour migration from Central, Eastern and South-Eastern Europe (CESEE) to EU and unemployment rates in recipient country, 2007–14

13.4 THE FUTURE OF CONVERGENCE

Will convergence continue? To close the income gap, countries in CEE will need to work more – or work better. There is less scope to work more. Since the turn of the millennium, employment rates have increased sharply, particularly in countries where the working-age population has declined (Figure 13.6). In many CEE countries, the employment rate is now above the EU15 average (66 per cent).

13.5 CONTINUED CONVERGENCE WILL REQUIRE RISING PRODUCTIVITY

Productivity has increased. Most CEE countries have seen a sharp convergence of productivity levels over the past decade.[2] In 2004, only a third of CEE countries had labour productivity above 60 per cent that of Germany; by 2015 this had increased to two-thirds (Figure 13.7).

The gap, however, remains wide, ranging from 20 per cent in Slovakia to 60 per cent in Albania. The gap is even wider when we look at productivity per hour rather than per worker. By this measure, the most productive country, Slovakia, is only 62 per cent as productive as Germany. Assessing

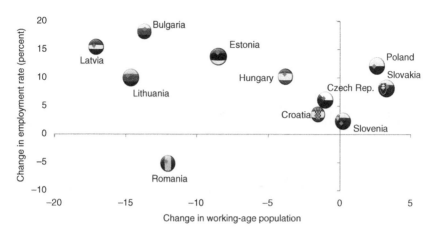

Note: 2001–14 for Croatia.

Sources: AMECO (Annual macro-economic) database of the European Commission, Eurostat and authors' calculations.

Figure 13.6 *Changes in employment rate and working-age population in the 'new' EU member states, 2000–14*

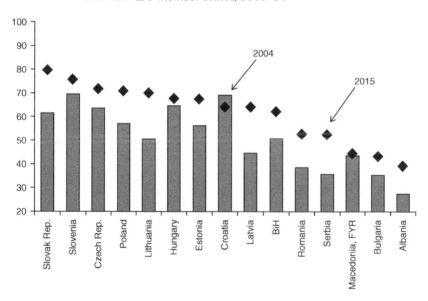

Sources: Total Economy Database (Conference Board) and authors' calculations.

Figure 13.7 *Labour productivity in Central and Eastern Europe (% of productivity per worker in Germany)*

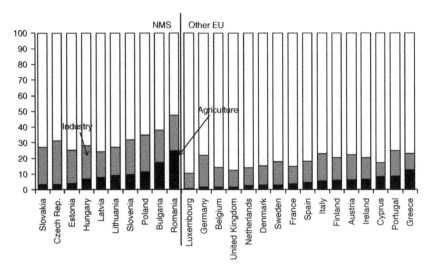

Sources: Eurostat and authors' calculations.

Figure 13.8   Structure of employment in the EU, 2014 (%)

productivity against global benchmarks, the gap in CEE is even wider. Hourly productivity levels in Slovakia are 41 per cent below those in the United States (US).

While further progress is expected, productivity convergence is likely to slow down as countries grow richer. Three of the most productive economies in 2004 closed the gap against Germany by only one percentage point until 2015.

Productivity would be boosted by structural transformation and reallocation of labour. The employment structure in CEE is still different from that in Western Europe, with a much higher share of employment in agriculture. Boosting productivity in agriculture, and transferring labour to more productive sectors, would boost overall productivity in the economy (Figure 13.8).

13.6   AGEING

Ageing will not just depress GDP growth, but also GDP per capita growth. With fertility rates well below replacement rates, the population in CEE is set to shrink further.[3] In the near term, the most important impact of ageing, however, will not be the decline of the population, but the

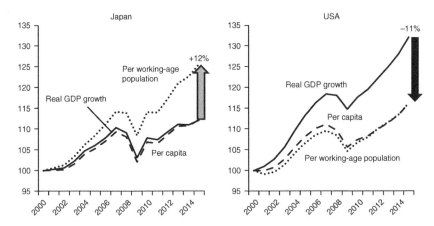

Sources: WEO (World Economic Outlook) database of the IMF, UN Total Population database and authors' calculations.

Figure 13.9 Real GDP in USA and Japan (index, 2000 = 100)

retirement of the working-age population. As a result, the working-age population – and thus the available source of labour – will decline much faster than the overall population. If the employment to working-age ratio and productivity remains constant, this will lead to a fall in GDP per capita.

A comparison of Japan with the US shows how powerful the impact of ageing could be. GDP in the US increased by 32 per cent between 2000 and 2015, almost three times as fast as in Japan (Figure 13.9). However, though other factors matter, a substantial part of the difference was the result of faster population growth – in terms of GDP per capita the difference in the annual average growth rate was only 0.2 percentage points. If we compare growth of GDP per working-age (15–64) capita, Japan actually appears to have grown much faster than the US. The working-age population in Japan is declining by almost 1 per cent a year, much faster than the decline of the population.[4]

According to United Nations (UN) population projections, in the next 15 years most CEE countries will see a sharper decline of their population than experienced by Japan in the last 15 years, that is, since the turn of the millennium. Moreover, the decline of the working-age population will be faster than the decline of the overall population (Figure 13.10).

As a result, during 2016–2020, population ageing will subtract some 0.7 percentage points from annual GDP per capita growth (Figure 13.11). A decomposition of real GDP per capita growth in the CEE region[5] suggests

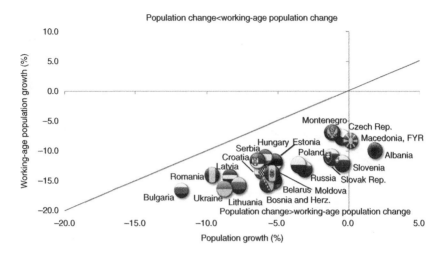

Sources: UN Total Population database and authors' calculations.

*Figure 13.10   Population and working-age population growth in Central,
Eastern and South-Eastern Europe, 2016–30*

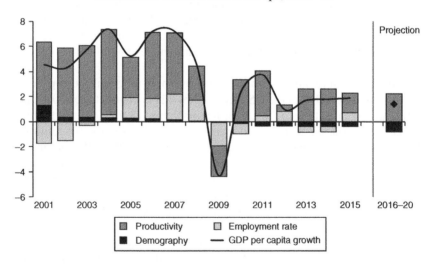

Note: Excludes Kosovo, Montenegro and Russia.

Sources: WEO (World Economic Outlook) database of the IMF, UN Total Population
database and authors' calculations.

*Figure 13.11   Real GDP per capita growth and its components in CESEE
(%)*

that the contribution of demographic factors turned negative in 2009, but this was partly offset by increasing employment rates. In most countries, there is some scope for further increases in employment rates, but it will become increasingly hard to offset the negative impact of demographic trends.

Without a pick-up in productivity growth or increasing employment rates, GDP growth will be modest at best. If we assume that productivity growth in CESEE (excluding Russia) in the next five years – that is, during 2016–2020 – will grow at the same rate as in the past five years (2.2 per cent) and that employment rates will remain flat, GDP per capita growth will be around 1.5 per cent only, and overall GDP growth close to only 1 per cent annually, 0.75 percentage points lower than in the past five years. Of course, higher growth rates are possible; but they require either higher productivity growth rates, or further increases in employment rates.

13.7 CONCLUSION

Since the turn of the millennium, there has been strong convergence of income levels between Eastern and Western Europe, but going forward, continued convergence may become more challenging. Much of the 'low-hanging fruit' has been picked; productivity levels are no longer at very low levels; and employment rates, which were very low, have increased sharply. Thus, going forward, raising productivity levels will not be as easy, while the scope for further increasing employment rate increases is more limited. In addition, demographic effects will dampen GDP per capita growth. That does not mean that convergence will not continue. But it will require strong policies: to boost labour force participation and employment rates, to further transform the structure of the economy, and to boost productivity levels.

NOTES

*	The views expressed in this chapter are those of the authors and do not necessarily represent the views of the International Monetary Fund (IMF), its Executive Board, or IMF management.
1.	Baltics: Estonia, Latvia, Lithuania. CE5: Czech Republic, Hungary, Poland, Slovakia, Slovenia. SEE EU: Bulgaria, Croatia, Romania. SEE non-EU: Albania, Bosnia and Herzegovina, Kosovo, FYR of Macedonia, Montenegro, Serbia. CEE consists of all the above plus Belarus, Moldova, Russia and Ukraine. EU-15: Austria, Belgium, Denmark, Finland, France, Germany, Greece, Ireland, Italy, Luxembourg, Netherlands, Portugal, Spain, Sweden, United Kingdom.

2. With the notable exception of some SEE countries (compared to Germany, relative productivity declined in Croatia and improved only marginally in Macedonia).
3. Continued emigration could further contribute to the decline.
4. However, more older people work in Japan, leaving the level of GDP per worker still well below that of the US.
5. Excluding Kosovo, Montenegro and Russia.

14. EU and CEE: productivity and convergence

Boris Vujčić

Since the 1990s, Central and Eastern European (CEE) countries have gone through significant institutional and economic transition and most of them are now full members of the European Union (EU). Nonetheless, their economic convergence is far from over, while income and productivity gaps between Central and Eastern Europe and 'old' Europe have not closed yet. Moreover, it seems that, since the onset of the global financial crisis in 2008, the convergence progress has slowed down. Faced with post-crisis challenges, the CEE countries will have to find new and more flexible drivers to support the relaunch of the catching-up process and to build more efficient and productive economic systems in years to come. So, in this chapter I review what has been achieved so far, and look into where potentials for further improvement of the CEE economies lie.

14.1 THE IMPORTANCE OF PRODUCTIVITY FOR THE RELATIVE POSITION OF A COUNTRY

The performance of the Central and Eastern EU member countries since the 1990s has been outstanding, making them a key driver of growth in Europe, and the only converging story in Europe. CEE countries started with a low level of productivity compared to old Europe. That was still the case even ten years into the transition. The productivity level was only half of the old Europe average in 2002 (Figure 14.1). However, convergence was very quick, and productivity growth demonstrates just how fast this progress was. Since the early 2000s, productivity growth in Central and Eastern Europe was on average more than three times higher than in the rest of the EU (Figure 14.2). To a large extent that was due to a dismal performance of old Europe, which has seen barely any increases in productivity. This catch-up process has slowed down somewhat during the crisis, but is still in place.

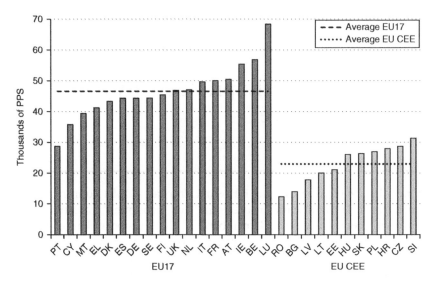

Note: AT = Austria. BE = Belgium. BG = Bulgaria. CY = Cyprus. CZ = Czech Republic. DE = Germany. DK = Denmark. EE = Estonia. ES = Spain. FI = Finland. FR = France. GR = Greece. HR = Croatia. HU = Hungary. IE = Ireland. IT = Italy. LT = Lithuania. LU = Luxembourg. LV = Latvia. MT = Malta. NL = Netherlands. PL = Poland. PT = Portugal. RO = Romania. SE = Sweden. SK = Slovakia. SI = Slovenia. UK = United Kingdom.

Source: Eurostat.

Figure 14.1   Labour productivity levels, 2002, in thousands of purchasing power standards (PPS)

On the other hand, misallocation of resources remains a potential issue among EU countries. According to evidence published by the Competitiveness Research Network (CompNet 2014) of the European Central Bank (ECB), productivity was very heterogeneous across firms operating within narrowly defined sectors, and distribution was not only disperse but also very asymmetric, featuring a large mass of low-productivity firms and very few high-productivity firms (Lopez-Garcia et al. 2015). According to available data for the CEE countries, Slovenia is among the countries with a better labour productivity distribution, while at the other end, Romania has a significant cluster of firms in the low-productivity area. Therefore, the data demonstrate significant potential for further increases in efficiency that can come from within-sector realloca-tion towards more-productive firms that can generate further productivity gains.

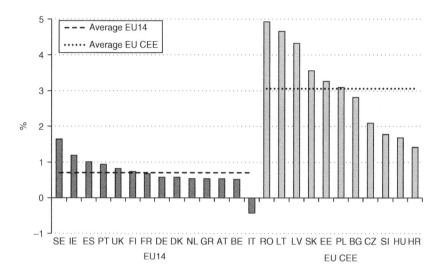

Note: AT = Austria. BE = Belgium. BG = Bulgaria. CZ = Czech Republic. DE =
Germany. DK = Denmark. EE = Estonia. ES = Spain. FI = Finland. FR = France. GR
= Greece. HR = Croatia. HU = Hungary. IE = Ireland. IT = Italy. LT = Lithuania. LV =
Latvia. NL =Netherlands. PL = Poland. PT = Portugal. RO = Romania. SE = Sweden. SK
= Slovakia. SI = Slovenia. UK = United Kingdom.

Source: Eurostat.

*Figure 14.2   Real labour productivity growth per person employed, average
annual % change, 2002–13*

14.2   WHERE DOES THE EU STAND COMPARED TO THE US?

Using the old EU as the benchmark for the CEE countries is motivated by
its role as the major economic and trade partner of the CEE economies,
as well as by the objective of creating a fully converged common currency
area. On the other hand, the United States (US) has, since the Second
World War, been used as a benchmark for the convergence of Europe, as
well as of the rest of the world. The crisis has revealed many of the structural and institutional weaknesses of the old EU. However, Europe's convergence progress towards the US actually stopped long before the crisis,
in the mid-1990s. In the early 2000s, US productivity growth re-accelerated
and the US–Europe gap widened. Today, old Europe stands at approximately 75 per cent of the US gross domestic product (GDP) per capita
level (Figure 14.3), the same relation as CEE countries towards old Europe.

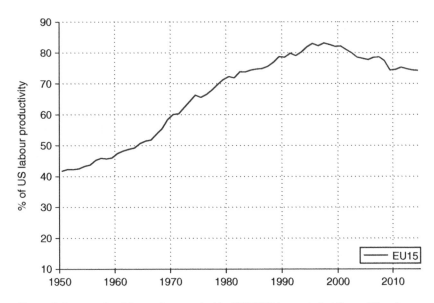

Note: Labour productivity per hour worked in 1990 US$ (converted at Geary–Khamis international dollar purchasing power parity) (US = 100).

Source: Total Economy Database, Conference Board (2015).

Figure 14.3   EU15 labour productivity

There is a large strand of literature trying to explain the differences in productivity between the US and Europe, and much emphasis has been put on the information and communication technology (ICT) revolution. It has been argued that the reason for higher productivity growth in the US lies in the ICT contribution and the amount of investment in the ICT industry. According to the data, there is a significant difference in investment in ICT and the contribution of ICT and total factor productivity to the US increase in productivity compared to that of the EU (Figure 14.4). Also, interesting research done by Bartelsman et al. (2010) shows that inflexible labour markets are not conducive to the growth of the ICT industry. In that sense, doing business, as measured for example by labour market flexibility but also by other indicators, is important for productivity growth. Fast-changing industries like ICT are prone to shocks and need to have flexible conditions for hiring and firing. Thus, they will refrain from setting up their business in countries with overly regulated labour markets. This research shows that there are differences between the flexibility of labour markets in the US and Europe, but also significant differences within Europe, making them more or less attractive for ICT investments.

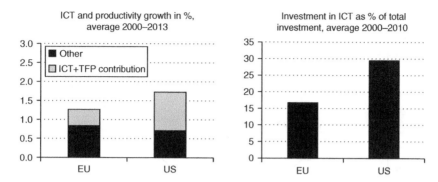

Notes: EU KLEMS stands for EU-level analysis of capital (K), labour (L), energy (E), materials (M) and service (S) inputs.

Sources: EU KLEMS; Conference Board; OECD.

Figure 14.4 ICT investments

Part of the explanation behind divergent productivity trends also lies in working habits. There are two trends here. The first is actually a favourable labour market trend in Europe that has served as a partial explanation of Europe's lagging behind in terms of productivity growth. Namely, since the mid-1990s Europe was converging towards the US in terms of increases in labour participation and employment, and that trend was present until the beginning of the crisis. After the breakout of the crisis, employment dropped in both the EU and the US, but at a much faster pace in the US. A few years into the crisis, however, it seems that the US and the EU are diverging again (Figure 14.5). Another crucial trend, but a less favourable one, is of the continued decline in working hours in Europe (Figure 14.6), both in absolute terms and relative to the US.

In addition, there are significant institutional differences between Europe and the US. According to 'Doing Business' data (Figure 14.7), the US is a place where the business environment is much more favourable than in old Europe, and CEE countries are lagging behind even more. Although CEE countries have done a lot since the beginning of their transition period, they improved their business environment even more in the post-crisis period. Nevertheless, this is an area where CEE countries can still do a lot and thus contribute to future catch-up with old Europe, and the US.

Europe is lagging behind in business momentum. In the 1990s, all large companies and all fast-growing companies were created in the US, not Europe. In addition, the evidence shows that US firms are more likely to expand or contract, while business in Europe is dominated by

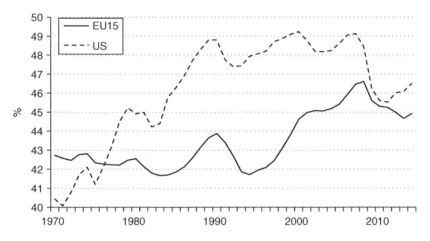

Note: The EU15 average is based on average monthly hours worked.

Source: Total Economy Database, Conference Board (2015).

Figure 14.5   Employment, % of the total population

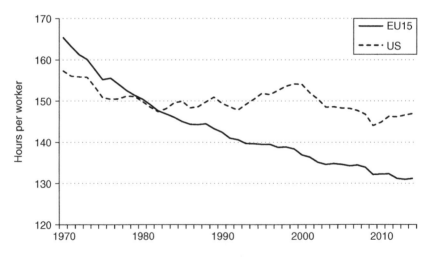

Note: The EU15 average is based on average monthly hours worked weighted by GDP
(converted at Geary–Khamis purchasing power parity).

Source: Total Economy Database, Conference Board (2015).

Figure 14.6   Average monthly hours worked per worker

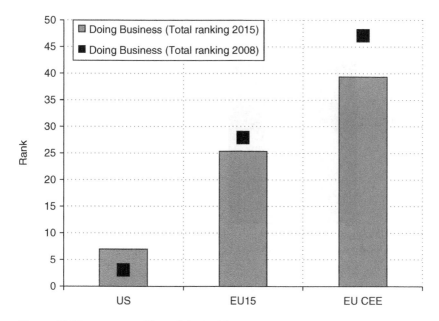

Notes: EU15 = average rankings of the 15 old EU members. EU CEE = average rankings of Central and Eastern European countries.

Sources: 'Doing Business' 2008 and 2015 (World Bank 2007, 2014).

Figure 14.7 Doing Business ranking

old static firms (Bravo-Biosca 2011). One can say that a Schumpeterian destruction works much better in the US than in Europe. Less-dynamic business growth distribution in Europe points to less experimentation and to a slower reallocation of resources from less- to more-productive businesses, two very important drivers of productivity growth. In addition, the higher proportion of static European firms suggests lower competitive pressures, which is potentially damaging for long-term productivity growth. As a result, the process of job reallocation across firms is slower, hampering productivity growth in Europe. Unfortunately, Europe has been unable to create an environment for fast-growing companies. That is something that should be a goal for Europe as a whole, not just for CEE.

Finally, in terms of financing conditions (Figure 14.8), we can see large differences in the availability of financing through equity and venture capital between the EU and the US. Young and prospective firms require access to financing sources in order to support their growth potential.

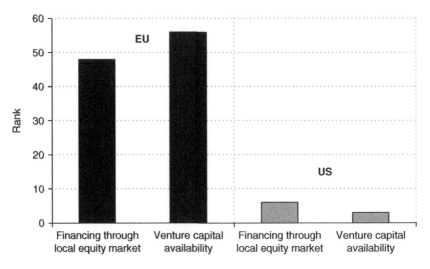

Note: EU rank = GDP weighted average of EU28 country rankings.

Source: World Economic Forum (2014).

Figure 14.8   Ranking according to access to finance.

Although this issue has been recognized in Europe, not much improvement is evident, except in rare cases such as the UK.

14.3   GOING FORWARD

One thing that has marked the change in the world landscape since the early 2000s is very rapid growth of productivity in emerging and developing economies. It was not only Central and East Europe catching up towards old Europe, but the whole emerging market world catching up to the mature economies, which has significantly increased competitive pressures. Productivity growth in emerging and developing economies reached its peak around 2007. Since then, mature and emerging economies have embarked on a slower trend of productivity growth. This slowdown, for emerging markets, appears to be a result of the end of a rapid catch-up growth period (Conference Board 2014, 2015).

Moreover, globalization and increased trade integration have reduced barriers to market access, and led to the relocation of the production. The relative price of tradable goods declined, which might have influenced the long-term trends in the inflation rates. A more intense global competition prevents companies from raising prices and puts downward pressures on wages in many sectors. This might partly explain the absence of the usual historical reaction of inflation rates to the unusually expansionary monetary policies that central banks are running these days. Globalization may have reduced the strength of the cyclical response of inflation to domestic output fluctuations. Prices of many items that are produced or consumed at home are increasingly determined by foreign demand and supply factors rather than local factors. Moreover, financial integration allows for larger trade balance deficits or surpluses and, thereby, weakens the relationship between domestic output and demand. However, in the globalized, more competitive world, countries with an absence of wage flexibility and/or productivity response experience a relative increase in unit labour costs (ULCs), which leads to an increase in unemployment rates, and/or increase in the public debt in the countries that decide to support weak sectors.

The crisis brought to an end the investment-driven growth model. The pre-crisis foreign capital inflows abruptly dried up, thus negatively affecting economic performance in the CEE region (Figure 14.9). In the post-crisis period, net foreign direct investment (FDI) inflows fell in all countries of the region. In the pre-crisis period Slovenia was the only exception, recording net outflows of international investments; all other countries were recipients of a strong inflow of FDIs (Figure 14.10). Post-crisis, along with the downward-heading investment cycle, the CEE region was also faced with excessive private sector leverage. Rapid debt build-up in the run-up

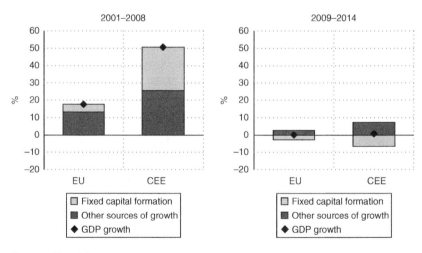

Source: Eurostat.

Figure 14.9   Investment contribution to GDP growth (%)

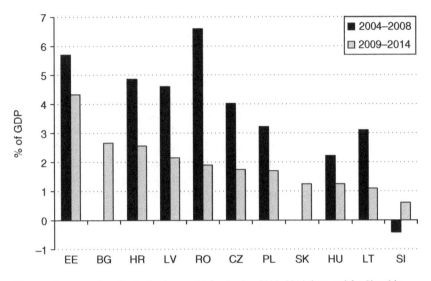

Notes: Average values for Bulgaria are obtained using 2010–2014 data and for Slovakia
using 2008–2014. Net liabilities are calculated as difference between liabilities and assets and
the positive sign refers to a net investment inflow. BG = Bulgaria. CZ = Czech Republic. EE
= Estonia. HR = Croatia. HU = Hungary. LT = Lithuania. LV = Latvia. PL = Poland. RO
= Romania. SI = Slovenia. SK = Slovakia.

Source: Eurostat.

Figure 14.10   *Direct investment: net incurrence of liabilities, average
2004–2008 and 2009–2014 (% of GDP)*

to the crisis raised concerns about the debt repayment possibilities during
the crisis, which triggered a deleveraging process in the post-crisis period.
Consequently, that has put an additional drag on investment recovery.
Only once the debt becomes sustainable and collateral rates increase can
we expect resumption in investment. Completion of the deleveraging
process is a necessary but not sufficient condition for restoring investment
growth. The CEE region clearly needs to find new investment drivers, and
they are more likely to be found domestically as the pre-crisis abundant
foreign capital inflows are unlikely to come back anytime soon (Dabrowski
2014). Hence, the key challenge for Central and Eastern Europe today is
to manage the transition from imported productivity gains to endogenous
sources of innovation as drivers of growth.

The question that arises is: what policy tools are available to relaunch
growth and convergence? Fiscal policy has been singled out by a number
of economists as the desirable policy tool to support economic recovery.
Yet, in reality, fiscal policy in the CEE region has behaved opposite to

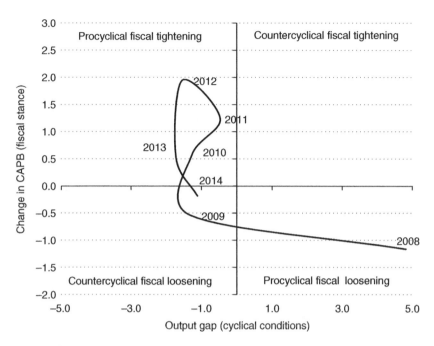

Note: The output gap and the change in the cyclically adjusted primary balance (CAPB) are computed as GDP-weighted averages of EU CEE countries. The impact of government assistance to the financial sector is excluded from the calculation of CAPB.

Sources: AMECO (Annual macro-economic) database, European Commission; Hrvatska narodna banka (HNB).

Figure 14.11 Cyclicality of fiscal policy

what would have been a desirable policy path. Fiscal policy was highly procyclical: expansionary before the crisis, while tightening in the midst of the crisis (Figure 14.11). So, why have countries not adjusted their fiscal policies to a more desirable stance? The answer is simple: because they had no fiscal space to do so. If you were in a wrong position in good times, you will end up being in a wrong position in bad times. Which is very similar to the macroprudential policy stance. After years of expansionary poli- cies that resulted in the build-up of high deficits and public debts, when the crisis struck, countries had no fiscal space to implement proactive countercyclical fiscal policies. High debt ratios now inevitably have to be sweated down and need to be brought to more sustainable levels. Except for the Baltics, none of the CEE members of the EU have yet reached their medium-term objectives (MTOs) set by the European Commission

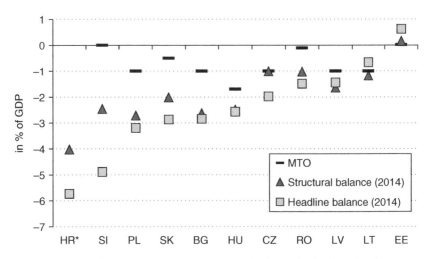

Notes: The MTO for Croatia is yet to be determined. BG = Bulgaria. CZ = Czech
Republic. EE = Estonia. HR = Croatia. HU = Hungary. LT = Lithuania. LV = Latvia. PL
= Poland. RO = Romania. SI = Slovenia. SK = Slovakia.

Sources: Eurostat; European Commission.

Figure 14.12   Medium-term objectives (MTO)

(Figure 14.12). In other words, if the fiscal Growth and Stability Pact is
enforced, public spending cannot be the driver of future growth, at least
not in the medium term. Therefore, the investment rebound will have to
come mainly from private sources, rather than through the fiscal space.

On top of the challenges mentioned above, there is also a serious longer-
term problem: the ageing of the population. It is a broader European
(and not only European) problem, but the population is ageing faster in
Central and Eastern Europe than in old Europe, which makes it especially acute in CEE. The old-age dependency ratio will double until 2060
in many countries (Figure 14.13). This will not only put more weight on
the growth prospects, but will also create additional pressure on the fiscal
position of all countries, although at varying degrees. In order to address
these challenges, the authorities will have to rethink the compatibility of
their labour market, pension and health care systems with demographic
trends. Measures to increase the labour force participation rates seem to be
an obvious, desirable, policy venue, alongside reforms of the pension and
health care systems.

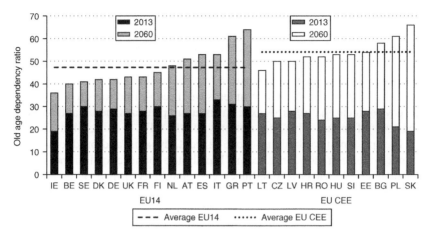

Notes: People aged 65 or above as % of the population aged 15–64. AT = Austria. BE = Belgium. BG = Bulgaria. CY = Cyprus. CZ = Czech Republic. DE = Germany. DK = Denmark. EE = Estonia. ES = Spain. FI = Finland. FR = France. GR = Greece. HR = Croatia. HU = Hungary. IE = Ireland. IT = Italy. LT = Lithuania. LU = Luxembourg. LV = Latvia. MT = Malta. NL =Netherlands. PL = Poland. PT = Portugal. RO = Romania. SE = Sweden. SK = Slovakia. SI = Slovenia. UK = United Kingdom.

Source: European Commission (2014).

Figure 14.13 Economic old-age dependency ratio (15–64)

14.4 CONCLUDING REMARKS

With the limited space for fiscal and monetary policies, the key priority for the CEE region is embarking on deep structural reforms. Monetary policy might have already done enough, if not too much. Furthermore, there is little or no fiscal space in most of the countries, particularly given the monetary policy constraints, to support cheap government financing in the long run. A too-long period of extremely low interest rates might become counterproductive, as it might induce more savings rather than spending. Therefore, the CEE region needs to continue with reforms that increase the productivity of domestic economies, and in particular with 'Doing Business' reforms aimed at reducing the complexity and cost of complying with business regulation and strengthening legal institutions, as well as improving overall efficiency of the public sector.

To conclude, over the next decade CEE will have to move from classical catching-up by imitation and imported productivity gains to a more flexible and knowledge-based system with more value added and more diversified exports. The CEE countries will need to further increase productivity of capital and labour by their own means, which makes investments in education, ICT and research and development (R&D) crucial. Fiscal policies will need to be directed toward restoring sustainability, while macroprudential measures should aim at safeguarding financial stability and avoiding recurrence of bubble episodes. Governments will need to find ways to encourage an environment that rewards experimentation, penalizes inertia and reduces the costs of failure. This goes not only for the CEE countries, but also for all Europe, aiming at building more efficient, dynamic and productive economic systems in the years to come. Finally, the countries of Europe, and in particular CEE, will have to rethink the compatibility of their labour market, pension and health care systems with the slowly but surely arriving challenge of a rapidly ageing population. That will almost certainly have to lead to the sorts of policies supportive of an increase in labour force participation.

REFERENCES

Bartelsman, E.J., A.G. Pieter and J. de Wind (2010), 'Employment Protection, Technology Choice, and Worker Allocation', IZA Discussion Paper 4895, Bonn: Institute for the Study of Labor (IZA).

Bravo-Biosca, A. (2011), 'A Look at Business Growth and Contraction in Europe', 3rd European Conference on Corporate R&D and Innovation, Nesta Working Paper 11/02, London: Nesta.

CompNet Task Force (2014), 'Micro-Based Evidence of EU Competitiveness: The CompNet Database', European Central Bank Working Paper Series 1634.

Conference Board (2014), '2014 Productivity Brief. Key Findings: Global Productivity Slowdown Moderated in 2013. 2014 May See Better Performance', New York: Conference Board.

Conference Board (2015), 'Productivity Brief 2015. Global Productivity Growth Stuck in the Slow Lane with No Signs of Recovery in Sight', New York: Conference Board.

Dabrowski, M. (2014), 'Central and Eastern Europe: uncertain prospects of economic Europe', Bruegel Institute, blog post, December 10: http://bruegel.org/2014/12/central-and-eastern-europe-uncertain-prospects-of-economic-convergence/.

European Commission (2014), 'The 2015 Ageing Report – Underlying Assumptions and Projection Methodologies', European Economy 8/2014.

Lopez-Garcia P., F. di Mauro and the CompNet Task Force (2015), 'Assessing European Competitiveness: The New CompNet Micro-based Database', European Central Bank Working Paper Series 1764.

World Bank (2007), 'Doing Business 2008', Washington, DC: World Bank Group.

World Bank (2014), 'Doing Business 2015. Going Beyond Efficiency', Washington, DC: World Bank Group.

World Economic Forum (2014), *The Global Competitiveness Report 2014–2015*, edited by K. Schwab, Geneva: World Economic Forum.

15. Peering into the crystal ball: can the CESEE countries be an engine of growth for the EU?

Iain Begg

After the remarkable transformation of the previous quarter of a century, the countries of Central, Eastern and Southeastern Europe (CESEE) have, arguably, reached a stage at which they have the potential to play a pivotal role in the development of the EU economy. Despite episodes of economic turmoil in some of them, their relative economic weight has grown since 2004 when eight of the CESEE countries acceded to the EU, and the comparative stagnation of much of Southern Europe over recent years should see further shifts in this direction.

Given their relative increase in economic weight, could CESEE be an engine of growth for the EU as a whole and, if so, how? One answer is simply through a demand channel: there is still scope for catch-up growth, particularly if the more rural areas converge on the capital regions which have, hitherto, tended to perform best. But for CESEE countries to add momentum to growth in the European Union (EU), they will need to shift to a model of growth that goes beyond catch-up. Further channels that could be influential are through a shift towards more innovation-driven growth and, in time, becoming a source of foreign direct investment. For CESEE countries to change from being a destination for foreign direct investment (FDI) to a source of it – perhaps emulating China which, in turn, is following in the footsteps of Korea and Japan – far-reaching shifts in the nature of economic development would be required. From this perspective, the sources of competitiveness warrant examination.

This chapter argues that the scope for becoming an engine of growth cannot be adequately understood by looking at a narrow interpretation of growth performance in terms of current rates of increase of gross domestic product (GDP). Instead, the more interesting questions are around the means by which a transformation in models could happen. The chapter therefore examines some relevant influences, while also considering constraints and uncertainties.

15.1   A MORE COMPETITIVE CESEE

The sources of growth are many, but in two key areas – innovation and skilled labour – the challenges are considerable for many CESEE countries and even more daunting for others. In labour cost or real exchange rate terms, the CESEE countries can appear to be quite competitive, especially where lower nominal wages in high-productivity, export-orientated sectors confer substantial advantages. Yet relying on relatively low wages is not a recipe for long-run economic convergence, even though it has been a factor in attracting inward investment; instead, growth from within has to be accentuated.

However, as Figure 15.1 shows, the scale of investment in research and development (R&D) in CESEE countries lags a long way behind the EU target of 3 per cent of GDP set in the Europe 2020 strategy. Several of the countries of Northern and Western Europe (NWE) have now attained the target or are on track to reach it soon. But even in the best-performing regions in the Czech Republic (Jihovýchod, with 2.61 per cent) and Poland (the capital region, Mazowieckie, 1.38 per cent), the R&D rate

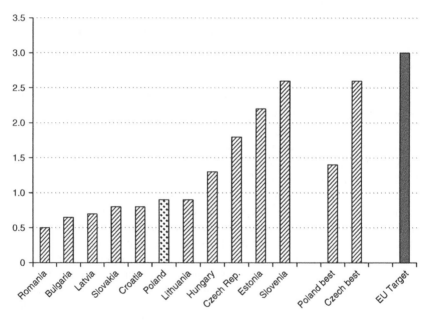

Source: Eurostat.

Figure 15.1   Investment in R&D in CESEE countries, 2012 (% of GDP)

is well below the target, and in some of the rural regions it is negligible. Given that manufacturing remains a larger share of the economy in most of these countries than in, for example, France or the United Kingdom (UK), where it is now under 10 per cent, the implication is that the bulk of European R&D-related innovation is being carried out elsewhere, and thus that CESEE countries are not well placed to be leaders in this regard.

The R&D data for Greece, Italy, Portugal and Spain show that these countries also lag well behind the NWE countries and show a similar lack of such investment in many of their less-developed regions. Thus, only Crete in Greece had an R&D investment rate above 1 per cent in 2012, while in Spain only the Basque region exceeds 2 per cent, and the best-performing region in Italy (Piemonte) attains only 1.9 per cent. However, even the worst-performing regions in Spain and Italy have R&D intensities well above the very low regional values seen in CESEE countries.

Skilled labour poses a similar problem. So long as qualified workers from CESEE are drawn to jobs in NWE ('brain drain'), two negative consequences can be expected. First, there is a risk that skill shortages in home countries will constrain growth potential, with the clear danger that the investment in education by CESEE will not be matched by the expansion of human capital. Second, if those emigrating do not have jobs that are commensurate with their skills and qualifications, there will be a risk of 'brain squandering', in the sense of individuals being unable to work to their personal potential. To some extent immigration from neighbouring states of the former Soviet Union offsets the first risk, but the risks that the balance will favour NWE to the detriment of CESEE is substantial. Bulgaria, for example, is confronted by such a large loss of working-age population that its economy faces acute difficulties in maintaining human capital.

A further, related concern is public investment which, as Figures 15.2 and 15.3 show, has declined since the crisis and is likely to remain constrained by pressures on public finances. In this regard, the CESEE countries look more positive, with all the top EU performers now from the region and attaining significantly higher rates than the rest of the EU, in contrast to the pre-crisis years.

The scope for becoming an engine of growth will be affected by a number of broader influences, both economic and political. Europe (the CESEE countries in particular) seems to lag behind the US in its capacity to foster the emergence of leading companies in the new, knowledge-based economy. The absence of a European Apple, Microsoft, Google or Facebook points to something lacking in Europe's innovation culture, and even those who point to the erstwhile success of Nokia have to reflect on why that success proved to be short-lived. A possible explanation is

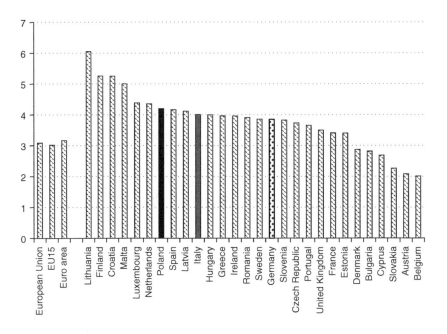

Source: AMECO (annual macroeconomic) database, European Commission.

Figure 15.2   Gross fixed capital formation: general government, 2002–07
            (% of GDP, annual average)

that, despite years of rhetoric about these industries – recall the (now, much derided) Lisbon strategy goal from March 2000 of making the EU the most dynamic, knowledge-based economy in the world by 2010 – too much of the policy thinking is attuned to an older conception of a division between industry and services.

A distinctive feature of the afore-mentioned large American companies is that they cannot easily be classified as manufacturers or service providers, precisely because they cut across these boundaries. They rely on creativity and content for added value, with the actual manufacturing outsourced to lower-income countries. The challenge for Europe is not just to improve the conditions for financing and growing new businesses, but also to rethink some of the underlying models of sectoral development. In the crystal ball, there are already signs that biotechnologies will have a profound effect in areas such as health care that, as with information and communication technologies (ICTs), cut across traditional boundaries.

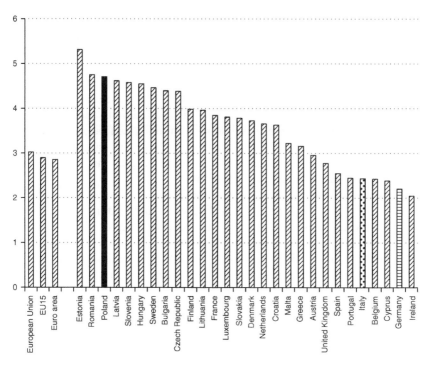

Source: European Commission, AMECO (Annual macro-economic) database.

Figure 15.3 Gross fixed capital formation: general government, 2011–15 (% of GDP, annual average)

15.2 SOURCES OF UNCERTAINTY

How the EU economy as a whole performs will also be important, yet must be seen as uncertain today. Even if it is accepted that the worst of the euro crisis is over, its legacy is likely to prove damaging in three respects that bear on EU growth and competitiveness. First, macroeconomic growth potential is likely to have diminished. In the 1980s, labour market analysts coined the term 'hysteresis' to describe the phenomenon of prolonged unemployment leading to diminished employability of affected workers, effectively shifting them from unemployment to being economically inactive. The extended period of stagnation and double or triple dips into recession may have had a similarly debilitating effect on the sources of productivity growth; this could be called 'innovation-hysteresis'. A second legacy is fragmentation of credit markets which, especially in Southern

Europe, may prolong a shortfall in investment and, in so doing, accentuate the division between the more dynamic and sluggish parts of the EU.

The third consequence is one that CESEE countries have already had to face, namely migration of skilled labour and the danger that human capital will be underused or even squandered. High unemployment rates in Spain, Portugal and Greece (especially for younger people) have seen an upsurge in labour mobility from these countries, as those able to move leave for better opportunities in NWE. While such mobility can be an important means of adjustment to an economic downturn, the danger is that it denudes origin countries or regions of the human capital that is likely to be crucial for further economic development.

This form of adjustment through mobility raises a tricky policy question. A period of employment in a different country, during which new skills or experiences are acquired, can be enriching for the individual worker. Just as technology transfer is recognized to be one of the sources of gains from inward direct investment, so labour mobility can contribute to human capital enhancement, but will only be beneficial to a worker's home country if they return after a period abroad.

The EU and, indirectly, the scope for CESEE countries to lead in Europe are also likely to be affected by the aftermath of current political tensions, notably around the future of the UK's relationship with the EU and the long-term consequences of the pressures on the Schengen area. Curbs on free movement are likely to add to operating costs and thus to inhibit the scope for further specialization either along product lines or along functional lines within production networks.

Despite the UK vote to leave the EU, the drift towards differentiated integration is likely to be accelerated. Nevertheless a strong message from the UK to the euro zone is that it has to integrate further to enable the euro to prosper. From the UK's perspective, this is a significant change of stance compared with resisting more integration, often arguing that this is about maintaining the integrity of the single market. Where it leads is hard to predict. The metaphor of 'two-speed Europe' implies travelling in the same direction, but with some member states reaching the destination faster than others, whereas what the UK wanted before the 'leave' result in the referendum can best be described as shallower integration.

The UK, however, has also sought to distinguish the euro zone from the rest of the EU, positing a clear separation between the interests of the 19 'ins' and the nine 'outs'. This, plainly, is a political source of uncertainty for CESEE. Despite the accession of five CESEE countries to the euro zone, enthusiasm to join the euro has clearly waned elsewhere as a result of the euro crisis and, looking into the crystal ball today, it is hard to see any rush to join in the next few years.

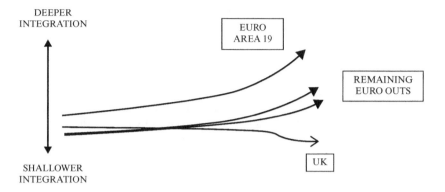

Figure 15.4   The UK's dilemma, but one others have to confront

Yet the UK position overlooks both divisions within the euro zone and the longer-term aspirations of countries like Poland, Hungary or the Czech Republic, all of which have strong supply network links to the core euro zone countries, especially Germany. Consolidation of banking union and adoption of at least some of the other forms of economic integration proposed by the 'Five Presidents'[1] to arrive at a more complete economic and monetary union will mean closer integration in the euro zone. But as the entrenched differences over common deposit insurance have shown, there are differing standpoints within the euro zone on how fast and how far to go towards deeper integration.

The dilemma for the six CESEE countries not in the euro zone (and, indeed, for Denmark and Sweden) is, consequently, whether (and how) to keep all options open, including by voluntary participation in some of the new mechanisms, or to gravitate towards the UK view. Figure 15.4 portrays the dilemma. In areas such as banking union or the competitiveness boards proposed in the Five Presidents' Report (European Commission 2015), rather than following the UK example, the interest of CESEE countries may be to participate to a greater or lesser degree in such integrating measures.

15.3   SHOULD WE EXPECT CESEE TO LEAD IN EUROPE?

'You can only predict things after they have happened' (Eugène Ionesco). Over the last few years, the CESEE countries have received a steady flow of support from what are now called the Structural and Investment Funds. Although sometimes regarded as redistributive policies (not least by the net contributors to the EU budget) these funds are not intended to, nor do they, redistribute incomes directly at the level of households. Instead, they underpin public investment. Together with other EU policies, they have helped to build up basic infrastructure, partly levelling the playing-field vis-à-vis competitor regions, and made some contribution to training. Of the other policy instruments at EU level, the European Fund for Strategic Investment (EFSI) is one which could be transformative by encouraging riskier investments in the private sector, as well as by further development of infrastructure networks. Poland is among the countries to have made the largest commitments to EFSI (perhaps surprisingly, so too did the UK, prior to the Brexit vote), suggesting that it intends to exploit the potential.

Having already undertaken some of the difficult structural reforms that the countries of Southern Europe are only now starting to confront, the relative dynamism of several of the CESEE countries is evident. They nevertheless need to acknowledge that the next stages of economic development will pose different challenges, and that making a further transition to a growth model based on innovation and an increased presence in the knowledge-based or creative industries will entail fresh policy thinking. Three dimensions of a strategy will be central to such a transition.

The first is adopting a coherent and comprehensive approach to innovation. The relatively low R&D intensity of most parts of CESEE, with only a few regions attaining rates of R&D investment comparable with NWE, suggests that one requirement will be to boost that investment. However, while more R&D can be thought of as a necessary condition, it is unlikely to be sufficient on its own. A complementary need will be to stimulate an innovation culture, to increase diffusion of good practices, and to ensure that appropriate financing is available for innovative activities. As part of this, an ambition will need to be to enhance the capabilities of research institutes and universities, such that they are able to cooperate more extensively with partners in NWE.

A second imperative will be to make CESEE more attractive to highly qualified workers, notably by enhancing the incentives to return to their home countries for the well-educated who have chosen to work in NWE. As the experience of the Irish diaspora has shown, this will not happen quickly, but the Irish example also shows that after the economy started to take off in the late 1980s, the flow of returning workers helped to sustain its growth. The delicate policy balance that CESEE countries need to strike is between facilitating further mobility and finding ways of luring back workers who have enhanced their human capital as described above.

Third, and perhaps a litmus test for success, will be whether the CESEE countries are able progressively to alter their position in supply chains and networks. By becoming the core of such networks, large German manufacturers have been able to sustain their position as market leaders, and there are similar configurations in retailing, banking and other financial services in which even banks incorporated in smaller EU countries such as Austria take the lead.

To sum up, there is a platform upon which the CESEE countries can build to increase their influence on the EU's economic trajectory, as well as in shaping the broad policy directions for European integration, but it cannot be taken for granted. Moreover, even if the comparatively higher growth in CESEE continues in the aftermath of the years of crisis, becoming a true engine of growth entails substantially more than having a better short- to medium-term macroeconomic performance.

NOTE

1. https://ec.europa.eu/priorities/sites/beta-political/files/5-presidents-report_en.pdf.

REFERENCE

European Commission (2015), 'The Five Presidents' Report: Completing Europe's Economic and Monetary Union', Report by Jean-Claude Juncker in close cooperation with Donald Tusk, Jeroen Dijsselbloem, Mario Draghi and Martin Schulz, Brussels.

Index

Printed and bound by CPI Group (UK) Ltd, Croydon, CR0 4YY

23/04/2025

14660979-0001